Get the Poem Outdoors

Get the poem outdoors under any pretext,
reach through the open window if you have to,
      kidnap it right off the poet's desk,
then walk the poem in the garden, hold it up
      among the soft yellow garlands of the
      willow,
command of it no further blackness, no silent
      cursing at midnight, no puny whimpering
      in the endless small hours, no more
      shivering in the cold-storage room of the
      winter heart,
tell it to sing again, loud and then louder so it
      brings the whole neighbourhood out, but
      who cares,
ask of it a more human face, a new tenderness,
      even the sentimental allowed between the
      hours of nine to five,
then let it go, stranger in a fresh green world, to
      wander down the flower beds, let it go to
      welcome each bird that lights on the still
      barren mulberry tree.

RAYMOND SOUSTER

Through the Open Window

Edited by

Shirley I. Paustian

Toronto   Oxford University Press   1983

Canadian Cataloguing in Publication Data

Main entry under title:
Through the open window

Includes index.
ISBN 0-19-540412-2

1. English poetry. 2. American poetry. 3. Canadian
poetry (English).* I. Paustian, Shirley Irene.

PN6101.T57   821'.008   C83-094199-1

© Oxford University Press (Canada) 1983

  23456789-98765

Design by Michael van Elsen Design Inc.
Cover photograph by Birgitte Nielsen

ISBN 0-19-540412-2

Printed in Canada

Table of Contents

Preface

Selecting poetry for an anthology is a little like taking a trip down the length of a mouth-watering buffet; before you have passed the salad bar you have already chosen more than enough to fill the available space! Fortunately poetry – the best of it – keeps well, and what must be left behind this time will still be there to be enjoyed at a later date.

The poetry in this book was chosen for you, the student. If you are already converted to poetry, so much the better. If not, perhaps you have not yet read enough poetry to realise that poems are not written for scholars and critics, but for all of us. They provide the lyrics for our favourite songs; they put into words the thoughts and feelings that perhaps could not be expressed in any other way; they make our everyday world new and vivid. Poetry is written for you. That is something you may never understand unless you meet, somewhere along the way, the poems that speak directly to you as an individual. Perhaps you will find them here.

Most of the poets represented in this book are British, Canadian or American, many famous, some not so famous. They offer a choice of poetry both traditional and modern from four centuries. The guiding purpose in making the selection has been to find poems that you, the student, will enjoy. If even a few of you who sample the food on the salad bar move on at a later date to enjoy the main course, this book will have served its purpose.

Shirley I. Paustian
1983

Acknowledgements

Suggestions and advice provided by English teachers in Ontario and in Alberta, and by members of the Language Arts Curriculum Committee for the Alberta Department of Education, are gratefully acknowledged. I am indebted to Arleen Ohlsen for assistance in research also, and to my husband for assistance with research and with the clerical aspects of the project, and for offering valuable support and criticism.

MILTON ACORN (1923-   ): Born in Charlottetown, P.E.I., he once described himself as a carpenter, a socialist, and a poet. He sold all his carpentry equipment to devote himself to poetry. Love of people and anger against social and political oppression are major themes in his poems, which he reads aloud and with great enthusiasm in cafés and at poetry readings around the country.

Charlottetown Harbor

An old docker with gutted cheeks,
time arrested in the used-up-knuckled hands
crossed on his lap, sits
in a spell of the glinting water.

He dreams of times in the cider sunlight
when masts stood up like stubble;
but now a gull cries, lights,
flounces its wings ornately, folds them,
and the waves slop among the weed-grown piles.

MILTON ACORN

Why a Carpenter Wears his Watch Inside the Wrist

They say it's guarded better
there, from the bumps of the trade.

I disproved this, and

guessed first those patched people
stuck up like chimneys
in high places, fix them
there so's to look at them
with no long upsetting armswing,
just a turn of the wrist,

but the gruesome truth is
that with the gargoyle-pussed
boss watching, they
don't worry much about balance;

which led me to the real reason
they wear watches tucked close
bouncing and scratching
among all their tools. . .

it's so they can look quick
out of the lefteyecorner
without the foreman seeing.

MILTON ACORN

FRANKLIN P. ADAMS (1881-1960): Born in Chicago, "FPA" was one of the great American wits of the twenties and thirties. After graduating in science and attempting to sell insurance, he turned to writing, notably journalism. He quickly became associated with other famous wisecrackers, including Dorothy Parker and Arthur Guiterman, who are represented in this anthology. He professed to dislike writing, saying that his real devotions were to his family and to tennis.

The Rich Man

The rich man has his motor-car,
  His country and his town estate.
He smokes a fifty-cent cigar
  And jeers at Fate.

He frivols through the livelong day,
  He knows not Poverty, her pinch.
His lot seems light, his heart seems gay;
  He has a cinch.

Yet though my lamp burns low and dim,
  Though I must slave for livelihood –
Think you that I would change with him?
  You bet I would!

FRANKLIN P. ADAMS

Fall

The geese flying south
In a row long and V-shaped
Pulling in winter.

SALLY ANDRESEN

A Few Limericks

There was an old fellow of Tyre,
Who constantly sat on the fire.
      When they asked, "Are you hot?"
      He replied, "No, I'm not.
I am James Winterbottom, Esq."

I sat next the duchess at tea.
It was just as I feared it would be.
      Her rumblings abdominal
      Were simply phenomenal,
And everyone thought it was me!

A girl who weighed many an oz.
Had a name that no one could pronoz.
Her brother, one day,
Pulled her chair right away.
He wanted to see if she'd boz.

There's a notable clan yclept Stein:
There's Gertrude, there's Ep, and there's Ein.
      Gert's prose has no style,
      Ep's statues are vile,
And nobody understands Ein.

A decrepit old gas man named Peter,
While hunting around for the meter,
      Scratched a match for a light
      And rose up out of sight,
And, as anyone can see by reading this, he also
      destroyed the metre.

ANONYMOUS

The Responsibility

I am the man who gives the word,
If it should come, to use the Bomb.

I am the man who spreads the word
From him to them if it should come.

I am the man who gets the word
From him who spreads the word from him.

I am the man who drops the Bomb
If ordered by the one who's heard
From him who merely spreads the word
The first one gives if it should come.

I am the man who loads the Bomb
That he must drop should orders come
From him who gets the word passed on
By one who waits to hear from him.

I am the man who makes the Bomb
That he must load for him to drop
If told by one who gets the word
From one who passes it from him.

I am the man who fills the till,
Who pays the tax, who foots the bill
That guarantees the Bomb he makes
For him to load for him to drop
If orders come from one who gets
The word passed on to him by one
Who waits to hear it from the man
Who gives the word to use the Bomb.

I am the man behind it all;
I am the one responsible.

PETER APPLETON

15

MARTIN ARMSTRONG (1882-1974): Born in England, he went from science to architecture to soldiering before turning to writing for a career. He married a Canadian, loved walking, gardening, and experiencing "the quality of human life as it is lived moment by moment." The poem Mrs. Reece Laughs *is a reflection of this latter interest.*

Mrs. Reece Laughs

Laughter, with us, is no great undertaking,
A sudden wave that breaks and dies in breaking.
Laughter with Mrs. Reece is much less simple:
It germinates, it spreads, dimple by dimple,
From small beginnings, things of easy girth,
To formidable redundancies of mirth.

Clusters of subterranean chuckles rise
And presently the circles of her eyes
Close into slits and all the woman heaves
As a great elm with all its mounds of leaves
Wallows before the storm. From hidden sources
A mustering of blind volcanic forces
Takes her and shakes her till she sobs and gapes.
Then all that load of bottled mirth escapes
In one wild crow, a lifting of huge hands,
And creaking stays, a visage that expands
In scarlet ridge and furrow. Thence collapse,
A hanging head, a feeble hand that flaps
An apron-end to stir an air and waft
A steaming face. And Mrs. Reece has laughed.

MARTIN ARMSTRONG

MARGARET ATWOOD (1939-   ): *Born in Ottawa, she is probably Canada's best known writer, both nationally and internationally. Alternating between writing and teaching at various universities in Canada, she has won a number of awards for her contributions to literature. There is a great sense of aloneness in much of her work, of separation, though recently she has dealt more with directly political or social topics. She speaks of the "magic" of poetry, not to express emotion ("If you want to express emotion, scream"), but to evoke emotion from the reader.*

Game After Supper

This is before electricity,
it is when there were porches.

On the sagging porch an old man
is rocking. The porch is wooden,

the house is wooden and grey;
in the living room which smells of
smoke and mildew, soon
the woman will light the kerosene lamp.

There is a barn but I am not in the barn;
there is an orchard too, gone bad,
its apples like soft cork
but I am not there either.

I am hiding in the long grass
with my two dead cousins,
the membrane grown already
across their throats.

We hear crickets and our own hearts
close to our ears;
though we giggle, we are afraid.

From the shadows around
the corner of the house
a tall man is coming to find us:

He will be an uncle,
if we are lucky.

MARGARET ATWOOD

Me As My Grandmother

Sometimes
I look up quickly
and see for an instant
her face
in my mirror,
random tightness
turns my mouth
into a facsimile of hers,
eyes caught oddly
in the glass
make me
into her
looking at me.

Now that she's dead,
I understand
that it is right
that I should age
and wrinkle into her.
It brings her back,
it puts me into
the cycle of family.
We look at all time
with just that
one same face.

ROSEMARY AUBERT

*W.H. AUDEN (1907-   ): Born in England and educated at
Oxford, he soon became associated with a group of young
Marxist poets in London, rebelling against the values of the
upper class he was born to. He married writer Erika Mann,
and in 1939 moved to the U.S.A. He has since influenced
many young American poets. It has been said that he has
the same "crazy wit" as e.e. cummings, "the same delight
in playing with words, and the same indifference as to
whether he is being understood." His skill in social criticism
is shown in all three poems represented here.*

The Average

His peasant parents killed themselves with toil
To let their darling leave a stingy soil
For any of those smart professions which
Encourage shallow breathing, and grow rich.

The pressure of their fond ambition made
Their shy and country-loving child afraid
No sensible career was good enough,
Only a hero could deserve such love.

So here he was without maps or supplies
A hundred miles from any decent town;
The desert glared into his blood-shot eyes;
The silence roared displeasure: looking down,
He saw the shadow of an Average Man
Attempting the exceptional, and ran.

W.H. AUDEN

The Unknown Citizen

(To JS/O7/M/378
This Marble Monument
is Erected by the State)

He was found by the Bureau of Statistics to be
One against whom there was no official complaint,
And all the reports on his conduct agree
That, in the modern sense of an old-fashioned word, he was
    a saint,
For in everything he did he served the Greater Community.
Except for the War till the day he retired
He worked in a factory and never got fired,
But satisfied his employers, Fudge Motors Inc.
Yet he wasn't a scab or odd in his views,
For his Union reports that he paid his dues,
(Our report on his Union shows it was sound)
And our Social Psychology workers found
That he was popular with his mates and liked a drink.
The Press are convinced that he bought a paper every day
And that his reactions to advertisements were normal
    in every way.
Policies taken out in his name prove that he was fully insured,
And his Health-card shows he was once in hospital but left
    it cured.
Both Producers Research and High-Grade Living declare
He was fully sensible to the advantages of the Instalment Plan
And had everything necessary to the Modern Man,
A phonograph, a radio, a car and a frigidaire.
Our researchers into Public Opinion are content
That he held the proper opinions for the time of year;
When there was peace, he was for peace; when there was
    war, he went.
He was married and added five children to the population,
Which our Eugenist says was the right number for a parent
    of his generation,
And our teachers report that he never interfered with their
    education.
Was he free? Was he happy? The question is absurd:
Had anything been wrong, we should certainly have heard.

W.H. AUDEN

Who's Who

A shilling life will give you all the facts:
How Father beat him, how he ran away,
What were the struggles of his youth, what acts
Made him the greatest figure of his day:
Of how he fought, fished, hunted, worked all night,
Though giddy, climbed new mountains; named a sea:
Some of the last researchers even write
Love made him weep pints like you and me.

With all his honours on, he sighed for one
Who, say astonished critics, lived at home;
Did little jobs about the house with skill
And nothing else; could whistle; would sit still
Or potter round the garden; answered some
Of his long marvellous letters but kept none.

W.H. AUDEN

PATRICK BARRINGTON (1908-   ): *Born in England of a noble family (he is Eleventh Viscount), he was at various times a barrister, a soldier, and a civil servant. But he is best known for his comic verse, much of which has been published in the English magazine* Punch.

I Had a Hippopotamus

I had a hippopotamus; I kept him in a shed
And fed him upon vitamins and vegetable bread;
I made him my companion on many cheery walks
And had his portrait done by a celebrity in chalks.

His charming eccentricities were known on every side,
The creature's popularity was wonderfully wide;
He frolicked with the Rector in a dozen friendly tussles,
Who could not but remark upon his hippopotamuscles.

If he should be afflicted by depression or the dumps,
By hippopotameasles or the hippopotamumps,
I never knew a particle of peace till it was plain
He was hippopotamasticating properly again.

I had a hippopotamus; I loved him as a friend;
But beautiful relationships are bound to have an end.
Time takes, alas! our joys from us and robs us of our blisses;
My hippopotamus turned out a hippopotamissis.

My housekeeper regarded him with jaundice in her eye;
She did not want a colony of hippopotami;
She borrowed a machine-gun from her soldier-nephew, Percy,
And showed my hippopotamus no hippopotamercy.

My house now lacks the glamour that the charming creature gave
The garage where I kept him is as silent as the grave;
No longer he displays among the motor-tires and spanners
His hippopotamastery of hippopotamanners.

No longer now he gambols in the orchard in the Spring;
No longer do I lead him through the village on a string;
No longer in the mornings does the neighbourhood rejoice
To his hippopotamusically-modulated voice.

I had a hippopotamus; but nothing upon earth
Is constant in its happiness or lasting in its mirth.
No joy that life can give me can be strong enough to smother
My sorrow for that might-have-been-a-hippopota-mother.

PATRICK BARRINGTON

STEPHEN VINCENT BENÉT (1898-1943): Born in Pennsylvania of a writing family, married to a writer, Benét never followed any profession but writing. His first book, six dramatic monologues in verse, was published when he was only seventeen. He had great talent for ballads, of which the emotionally patriotic John Brown's Body *is his most famous. He was in fact often criticized for his emotional approach to national concerns.*

The Ballad of William Sycamore

My father, he was a mountaineer,
His fist was a knotty hammer;
He was quick on his feet as a running deer,
And he spoke with a Yankee stammer.

My mother, she was merry and brave,
And so she came to her labor,
With a tall green fir for her doctor grave
And a stream for her comforting neighbor.

And some are wrapped in the linen fine,
And some like a godling's scion;
But I was cradled on twigs of pine
In the skin of a mountain lion.

And some remember a white, starched lap
And a ewer with silver handles;
But I remember a coonskin cap
And the smell of bayberry candles.

The cabin logs, with the bark still rough,
And my mother who laughed at trifles,
And the tall, lank visitors, brown as snuff,
With their long, straight squirrel-rifles.

I can hear them dance, like a foggy song,
Through the deepest one of my slumbers,
The fiddle squeaking the boots along
And my father calling the numbers.

The quick feet shaking the puncheon-floor,
The fiddle squeaking and squealing,
Till the dried herbs rattled above the door
And the dust went up to the ceiling.

There are children lucky from dawn till dusk,
But never a child so lucky!
For I cut my teeth on "Money Musk"
In the Bloody Ground of Kentucky!

When I grew tall as the Indian corn,
My father had little to lend me,
But he gave me his great, old powder-horn
And his woodsman's skill to befriend me.

With a leather shirt to cover my back,
And a redskin nose to unravel
Each forest sign, I carried my pack
As far as a scout could travel.

Till I lost my boyhood and found my wife,
A girl like a Salem clipper!
A woman straight as a hunting-knife
With eyes as bright as the Dipper!

We cleared our camp where the buffalo feed,
Unheard-of streams were our flagons;
And I sowed my sons like apple-seed
On the trail of the Western wagons.

They were right, tight boys, never sulky or slow,
A fruitful, a goodly muster.
The eldest died at the Alamo.
The youngest fell with Custer.

The letter that told it burned my hand.
Yet we smiled and said, "So be it!"
But I could not live when they fenced the land,
For it broke my heart to see it.

I saddled a red, unbroken colt
And rode him into the day there;

And he threw me down like a thunderbolt
And rolled on me as I lay there.

The hunter's whistle hummed in my ear
As the city-men tried to move me,
And I died in my boots like a pioneer
With the whole wide sky above me.

Now I lie in the heart of the fat, black soil,
Like the seed of a prairie-thistle;
It has washed my bones with honey and oil
And picked them clean as a whistle.

And my youth returns, like the rains of Spring,
And my sons, like the wild-geese flying;
And I lie and hear the meadow-lark sing
And have much content in my dying.

Go play with the towns you have built of blocks,
The towns where you would have bound me!
I sleep in my earth like a tired fox,
And my buffalo have found me.

STEPHEN VINCENT BENÉT

JOHN BETJEMAN (1906-   ), born in England, was a contem-
porary of W.H. Auden at Oxford. He has never been affiliated
with a "school" of poets. His life-long love affair with
Edwardian England has included old churches, old gaslit
streets, old people. He is at times a satirical poet, attacking
cruelty and, as in In Westminster Abbey, *hypocrisy and self-*
complacency. He is sometimes thought rather old-fashioned,
writing only of England in traditional styles, but his poems
show the great gentleness and good nature in his affection
for "ordinary" people.

In Westminster Abbey

Let me take this other glove off
   As the *vox humana* swells,
And the beauteous fields of Eden
   Bask beneath the Abbey bells.
Here, where England's statesmen lie,
Listen to a lady's cry.

Gracious Lord, oh bomb the Germans.
   Spare their women for Thy Sake,
And if that is not too easy
   We will pardon Thy Mistake.
But, gracious Lord, whate'er shall be,
Don't let anyone bomb me.

Keep our Empire undismembered
   Guide our Forces by Thy Hand,
Gallant blacks from far Jamaica,
   Honduras and Togoland;
Protect them Lord in all their fights,
And, even more, protect the whites.

Think of what our Nation stands for,
   Books from Boots' and country lanes,
Free speech, free passes, class distinction,
   Democracy and proper drains.
Lord, put beneath Thy special care
One-eighty-nine Cadogan Square.

Although dear Lord I am a sinner,
   I have done no major crime;

Now I'll come to Evening Service
    Whensoever I have time.
So, Lord, reserve for me a crown,
And do not let my shares go down.

I will labour for Thy Kingdom,
    Help our lads to win the war,
Send white feathers to the cowards
    Join the Women's Army Corps,

Then wash the Steps around Thy Throne
In the Eternal Safety Zone.

Now I feel a little better,
    What a treat to hear Thy Word,
Where the bones of leading statesmen,
    Have so often been interr'd.
And now, dear Lord, I cannot wait
Because I have a luncheon date.

JOHN BETJEMAN

WILLIAM BEYER (1911-   ) was born in Indiana, the son of a book-seller. He has been involved in literature all his life, as teacher, writer, critic and university professor. Married with two children, he is a keen traveller with a love of the outdoor life.

The Trap

"That red fox,
Back in the furthest field,
Caught in my hidden trap,
Was half mad with fear.
During the night
He must have ripped his foot
From the cold steel.
I saw him early this morning,
Dragging his hurt leg,
Bleeding a path across the gold wheat,
Whining with the pain;
His eyes like cracked marbles.
I followed as he moved,
His thin body pulled to one side
In a weird helplessness.
He hit the wire fence,
Pushing through it
Into the deep, morning corn,
And was gone."
The old man looked around the kitchen
To see if anyone was listening.
"Crazy red fox.
Will kill my chickens no longer.
Will die somewhere in hiding."
He lit the brown tobacco carefully,
Watching the blue smoke rise and disappear
In the movement of the air.
Scratching his red nose slowly,

Thinking something grave for a long moment,
He stared out of the bright window.
"He won't last long with that leg," he said.
The old man turned his head
To see if his wife was listening.
But she was deep in thought,
Her stained fingers
Pressing red berries in a pie.
He turned his white head
Toward the open window again.
"Guess I'll ride into the back field, first thing.
Some mighty big corn back there this year.
Mighty big corn."
His wife looked up from her work,
Smiled almost secretly to herself,
And finished packing the ripe berries
Into the pale crust.

WILLIAM BEYER

EARLE BIRNEY (1904-   ): Born in Calgary and brought up
in Alberta, he has had a varied career in the army, as a
university lecturer, and as an editor. He has written a great
deal and is known both in Canada and abroad. The range of
his social criticism includes exploitation of both people and
the environment. Birney says, "I believe that my poems are
the best proof I can print of my Humanness, signals out of
the loneliness into which all of us are born, and in which we
die, affirmations of kinship with all the other wayfarers."

Curaçao

I think I am going to love it here

I ask the man in the telegraph office
the way to the bank
He locks the door and walks with me
insisting he needs the exercise

When I ask the lady at my hotel desk
what bus to take to the beach
she gets me a lift with her beautiful sister
who is just driving by in a sports job

And already I have thought of something
I want to ask the sister

EARLE BIRNEY

Transcontinental

Crawling across this sometime garden
now in our trainbeds like clever nits
in a plush caterpillar should we take time
to glance from our dazzle of magazines
and behold this great green girl grown sick
with man   sick with the likes of us?

Toes mottled long ago by soak of seaports
ankles rashed with stubble
belly papulous with stumps?
And should we note where maggoting miners
still bore her bones to feed our crawling host
or consider the scars across her breasts
the scum of tugs upon her lakeblue eyes
the clogging logs within her blood –
in the doze between our magazines?

For certainly she is ill   her skin
is creased with our coming and going
and we trail in her face the dark breath of her dooming

She is too big and strong perhaps to die
of this disease but she grows quickly old
this lady   old with us –
nor have we any antibodies for her aid
except our own.

EARLE BIRNEY

David

David and I that summer cut trails on the Survey,
All week in the valley for wages, in air that was steeped
In the wail of mosquitoes, but over the sunalive week-
    ends
We climbed, to get from the ruck of the camp, the surly

Poker, the wrangling, the snoring under the fetid
Tents, and because we had joy in our lengthening
    coltish
Muscles, and mountains for David were made to see
    over,
Stairs from the valleys and steps to the sun's retreats.

II

Our first was Mount Gleam. We hiked in the long
    afternoon
To a curling lake and lost the lure of the faceted
Cone in the swell of its sprawling shoulders. Past
The inlet we grilled our bacon, the strips festooned

On a poplar prong, in the hurrying slant of the sunset.
Then the two of us rolled in the blanket while around us
    the cold
Pines thrust at the stars. The dawn was a floating
Of mists till we reached to the slopes above timber,
    and won

To snow like fire in the sunlight. The peak was
    upthrust
Like a fist in a frozen ocean of rock that swirled
Into valleys the moon could be rolled in. Remotely
    unfurling
Eastward the alien prairie glittered. Down through
    the dusty

Skree on the west we descended, and David showed me
How to use the give of shale for giant incredible
Strides. I remember, before the larches' edge,
That I jumped a long green surf of juniper flowing

33

Away from the wind, and landed in gentian and saxifrage
Spilled on the moss. Then the darkening firs
And the sudden whirring of water that knifed down a
    fern-hidden
Cliff and splashed unseen into mist in the shadows.

III

One Sunday on Rampart's arête a rainsquall caught us,
And passed, and we clung by our blueing fingers and
    bootnails
An endless hour in the sun, not daring to move
Till the ice had steamed from the slate. And David
    taught me

How time on a knife-edge can pass with the guessing of
    fragments
Remembered from poets, the naming of strata beside
    one,
And matching of stories from schooldays . . . We
    crawled astride
The peak to feast on the marching ranges flagged

By the fading shreds of the shattered stormcloud.
    Lingering
There it was David who spied to the south, remote,
And unmapped, a sunlit spire on Sawback, an overhang
Crooked like a talon. David named it the Finger.

That day we chanced on the skull and the splayed
    white ribs
Of a mountain goat underneath a cliff-face, caught
On a rock. Around were the silken feathers of hawks.
And that was the first I knew that a goat could slip.

IV

And then Inglismaldie. Now I remember only
The long ascent of the lonely valley, the live
Pine spirally scarred by lightning, the slicing pipe
Of invisible pika, and great prints, by the lowest

Snow, of a grizzly. There it was too that David
Taught me to read the scroll of coral in limestone
And the beetle-seal in the shale of ghostly trilobites,
Letters delivered to man from the Cambrian waves.

V

On Sundance we tried from the col and the going was
       hard.
The air howled from our feet to the smudged rocks
And the papery lake below. At an outthrust we balked
Till David clung with his left to a dint in the scarp,

Lobbed the iceaxe over the rocky lip,
Slipped from his holds and hung by the quivering pick,
Twisted his long legs up into space and kicked
To the crest. Then grinning, he reached with his
       freckled wrist

And drew me up after. We set a new time for that
       climb.
That day returning we found a robin gyrating
In grass, wing-broken. I caught it to tame but David
Took and killed it, and said, 'Could you teach it to
       fly?'

VI

In August, the second attempt, we ascended The
       Fortress.
By the forks of the Spray we caught five trout and fried
       them
Over a balsam fire. The woods were alive
With the vaulting of mule-deer and drenched with
       clouds all the morning,

Till we burst at noon to the flashing and floating round
Of the peaks. Coming down we picked in our hats the
       bright
And sunhot raspberries, eating them under a mighty
Spruce, while a marten moving like quicksilver scouted
       us.

VII

But always we talked of the Finger on Sawback,
    unknown
And hooked, till the first afternoon in September we
    slogged
Through the musky woods, past a swamp that quivered
    with frog-song,
And camped by a bottle-green lake. But under the cold

Breath of the glacier sleep would not come, the moon-
    light
Etching the Finger. We rose and trod past the
    feathery
Larch, while the stars went out, and the quiet heather
Flushed, and the skyline pulsed with the surging bloom

Of incredible dawn in the Rockies. David spotted
Bighorns across the moraine and sent them leaping
With yodels the ramparts redoubled and rolled to the
    peaks,
And the peaks to the sun. The ice in the morning thaw

Was a gurgling world of crystal and cold blue chasms,
And seracs that shone like frozen saltgreen waves.
At the base of the Finger we tried once and failed.
    Then David
Edged to the west and discovered the chimney; the last

Hundred feet we fought the rock and shouldered and
    kneed
Our way. For an hour and made it. Unroping we found
A cairn on the rotting tip. Then I turned to look north
At the glistening wedge of giant Assiniboine, heedless

Of handhold. And one foot gave. I swayed and
    shouted.
David turned sharp and reached out his arm and
    steadied me,
Turning again with a grin and his lips ready
To jest. But the strain crumbled his foothold. Without

A gasp he was gone. I froze to the sound of grating
Edge-nails and fingers, the slither of stones, the lone
Second of silence, the nightmare thud. Then only
The wind and the muted beat of unknowing cascades.

VIII

Somehow I worked down the fifty impossible feet
To the ledge, calling and getting no answer but echoes
Released in the cirque, and trying not to reflect
What an answer would mean. He lay still, with his
    lean

Young face upturned and strangely unmarred, but his
    legs
Splayed beneath him, beside the final drop,
Six hundred feet sheer to the ice. My throat stopped
When I reached him, for he was alive. He opened his
    grey

Straight eyes and brokenly murmured 'over . . . over.'
And I, feeling beneath him a cruel fang
Of the ledge thrust in his back, but not understanding,
Mumbled stupidly, 'Best not to move,' and spoke

Of his pain. But he said, 'I can't move . . . If only I felt
Some pain.' Then my shame stung the tears to my
    eyes
As I crouched, and I cursed myself, but he cried,
Louder, 'No, Bobbie! Don't ever blame yourself.

I didn't test my foothold.' He shut the lids
Of his eyes to the stare of the sky, while I moistened his
    lips
From our water flask and tearing my shirt into strips
I swabbed the shredded hands. But the blood slid

From his side and stained the stone and the thirsting
    lichens,
And yet I dared not lift him up from the gore
Of the rock. Then he whispered, 'Bob, I want to go
    over!'
This time I knew what he meant and I grasped for a lie

And said, 'I'll be back here by midnight with ropes
And men from the camp and we'll cradle you out.'
     But I knew
That the day and the night must pass and the cold dews
Of another morning before such men unknowing

The ways of mountains could win to the chimney's top.
And then, how long? And he knew . . . and the hell
     of hours
After that, if he lived till we came, roping him out.
But I curled beside him and whispered, 'The bleeding
     will stop.

You can last.' He said only, 'Perhaps . . . For
     what? A wheelchair,
Bob?' His eyes brightening with fever upbraided me.
I could not look at him more and said, 'Then I'll stay
With you.' But he did not speak, for the clouding
     fever.

I lay dazed and stared at the long valley,
The glistening hair of a creek on the rug stretched
By the firs, while the sun leaned round and flooded the
     ledge,
The moss, and David still as a broken doll.

I hunched to my knees to leave, but he called and his
     voice
Now was sharpened with fear. 'For Christ's sake push
     me over!
If I could move . . . Or die . . .' The sweat ran from
     his forehead,
But only his eyes moved. A hawk was buoying

Blackly its wings over the wrinkled ice.
The purr of a waterfall rose and sank with the wind.
Above us climbed the last joint of the Finger
Beckoning bleakly the wide indifferent sky.

Even then in the sun it grew cold lying there . . . And
     I knew

He had tested his holds. It was I who had not . . . I
      looked
At the blood on the ledge, and the far valley. I looked
At last in his eyes. He breathed, 'I'd do it for you, Bob.'

IX

I will not remember how nor why I could twist
Up the wind-devilled peak and down through the
      chimney's empty
Horror, and over the traverse alone. I remember
Only the pounding fear I would stumble on It

When I came to the grave-cold maw of the bergschrund
      . . . reeling
Over the sun-cankered snowbridge, shying the caves
In the névé . . . the fear, and the need to make sure
      It was there
On the ice, the running and falling and running,
      leaping

Of gaping greenthroated crevasses, alone and pursued
By the Finger's lengthening shadow. At last through
      the fanged
And blinding seracs I slid to the milky wrangling
Falls at the glacier's snout, through the rocks piled huge

On the humped moraine, and into the spectral larches,
Alone. By the glooming lake I sank and chilled
My mouth but I could not rest and stumbled still
To the valley, losing my way in the ragged marsh.

I was glad of the mire that covered the stains, on my
      ripped
Boots, of his blood, but panic was on me, the reek
Of the bog, the purple glimmer of toadstools obscene
In the twilight. I staggered clear to a firewaste,
      tripped

And fell with a shriek on my shoulder. It somehow
      eased
My heart to know I was hurt, but I did not faint

And I could not stop while over me hung the range
Of the Sawback. In blackness I searched for the trail
    by the creek

And found it . . . My feet squelched a slug and
    horror
Rose again in my nostrils. I hurled myself
Down the path. In the woods behind some animal
    yelped.
Then I saw the glimmer of tents and babbled my story.

I said that he fell straight to the ice where they found
    him.
And none but the sun and incurious clouds have
    lingered
Around the marks of that day on the ledge of the
    Finger,
That day, the last of my youth, on the last of our
    mountains.

EARLE BIRNEY

MORRIS BISHOP (1893-1973) was born in New York State, and attended Cornell University. He served in the First World War and later returned to Cornell as professor of Romance languages. His writings are mostly light verse and scholarly work.

Ambition

I got pocketed behind 7X-3824;
He was making 65, but I can do a little more.
I crowded him on the curves, but I couldn't get past,
And on the straightaways there was always some truck
    coming fast.
Then we got to the top of a mile-long incline
And I edged her out to the left, a little over the
    white line,
And ahead was a long grade with construction at the
    bottom,
And I said to the wife, "Now by golly I got 'm!"
I bet I did 85 going down the long grade,
And I braked her down hard in front of the barricade,
And I swung in ahead of him and landed fine
Behind 9W-7679.

MORRIS BISHOP

From "Songs of Innocence"

To see a world in a grain of sand
And a heaven in a wild flower
Hold infinity in the palm of your hand
And eternity in an hour.

WILLIAM BLAKE (1757-1827)

GEORGE BOWERING (1935-   ): Born in British Columbia, he served in the Royal Canadian Air Force, worked in forestry and agriculture, and has taught in various universities across the country. Bowering says, "I don't write personal poetry. In fact when personal poetry gets to be confessional poetry I turn it off and reach for the baseball scores." Bowering has written about an immense number of things because he was "all those things that other poets always are on the dust jackets before they became poets."

Albertasaurus

The great valley of Drumheller
a silent gorge, filled
with dinosaur bones,

unexpected trees on the plains,
old ghost towns of coal
mines & dinosaurs,

the wood, petrified, the earth
streakt white & brown,
the Badlands, sea shells

caught a thousand miles
from the sea. In the town
small-town cafés, restaurants
they say, with Pepsi-Cola neon
signs, old-fashioned menus,

the home of the dinosaur,
caught in the corner of the
prairie, small-town people

in a dying town, conscious
they must cling to the
dinosaur for their living,

cling to his neck, forgetting
where the dinosaur came
to rest.

GEORGE BOWERING

News

Every day I add an inch
to the pile of old newspapers
in the closet.

In that three foot pile now
a dozen airliner crashes,
one earthquake in Alaska,
seventeen American soldiers
face down in Asian mud

I could go on enumerating
like newsprint – we record
violent death & hockey scores
& keep the front room neat.

In front of me, on the table
my empty coffee cup, somewhat melted
butter, carbon copy of an old poem,
familiar things, nothing unexpected.

A plane could crash into the kitchen –
a fissure could jag the floor open –
some olive faced paratrooper bash
his rifle butt thru the window –

It would be news, somewhere.

GEORGE BOWERING

*ELIZABETH BREWSTER (1922-   ): Born in New Brunswick,
she attended the universities of New Brunswick, London,
Toronto, and Indiana. She has published several volumes of
verse written in a natural and direct style, and she has served
as librarian and teacher in many universities. Much of her
poetry deals with environment and people in relation to each
other and to herself. She constantly tries to find in the people
and places she has known some permanent values amid the
changefulness of present society.*

Blueflag

So that I would not pick the blueflag
in the midst of the pond
(and get my clothes wet)
my mother told me that it was poison.

I watched this beautiful, frightening flower
growing up from the water
from its green reeds,
washed blue, sunveined,
and wanted it more
than all the flowers I was allowed to pick,
wild roses, pink and smooth as soap,
or the milk-thin daisies
with butterblob centres.

I noticed that the midges
that covered the surface of the water
were not poisoned by the blueflag,
but I thought they must have
a different kind of life from mine.

Even now, if I pick one,
fear comes over me, a trembling.
I half expect to be struck dead
by the flower's magic

a potency seeping
from its dangerous blue skin
its veined centre.

ELIZABETH BREWSTER

The Night Grandma Died

"Here's Grandmother in here," Cousin Joy said,
Standing beside me at the bedroom door,
One hand on my shoulder. "You see, she's only sleeping."
But I, nine years old and frightened,
Knew it was a lie. Grandmother's shell
Lay on the bed, hands folded, head on one side,
The spirit that had groaned so loud an hour ago
Gone out of her. I looked, and turned and ran,
First to the kitchen. There were the aunts
Who had laid her out, still weeping
Over a good hot cup of tea: Aunt Stella,
Large, dominant; Aunt Alice, a plump, ruffled hen of a woman;
My small, quick mother; Aunt Grace, youngest and shyest,
Awkward on the edge of the group: "Shush," she was saying
To Cousin Pauline, who was lying on the floor
Pretending to be Grandma.

And they all got up and came into the parlour,
Where suddenly everyone was jovial,
And Aunt April sat in the best chair
Nursing her newest baby,
And the uncles sat talking of crops and weather,
And Uncle Harry, who had come from Maine,
Pumped the hands of people he hadn't seen in twenty years,
And Grandma's nephew Eb from up the road
Played everybody's favourite tune on the piano.
Now and then, remembering the corpse, he burst into a Baptist hymn,
His rich bass voice, dark and deep as molasses,
Flowing protectively over the women,
While his eyes, also dark,
Wrapped them warm with sympathy.

And I, sitting on a footstool in a corner,
Was sometimes warmed by the voice,
And sometimes chilled remembering
In the room next door
Grandmother, dead, whom I had never liked.

ELIZABETH BREWSTER

*EDWIN BROCK (1927-   ) was born in England of working-
class parents in South London. Much of Brock's poetry is
about his family relationships, his marriages, his children.
He has worked in publishing and as a police constable, but he
says that "poetry is the nearest thing to an activity I have yet
found. This statement [is] not as flip as it sounds: I believe
that most activity is an attempt to define oneself in one way
or another: for me poetry, and only poetry, has provided this
self-defining act."*

A Moment of Respect

Two things I remember about my grandfather:
his threadbare trousers, and the way he adjusted
his half-hunter watch two minutes every day.

When I asked him why he needed to know the time so
exactly, he said a business man could lose a fortune
by being two minutes late for an appointment.

When he died he left two meerschaum pipes
and a golden sovereign on a chain. Somebody
threw the meerschaum pipes away, and
there was an argument about the sovereign.

On the day of his burial the church clock chimed
as he was lowered down into the clay, and all
the family advanced their watches by two minutes.

EDWIN BROCK

Five Ways to Kill a Man

There are many cumbersome ways to kill a man:
you can make him carry a plank of wood
to the top of a hill and nail him to it. To do this
properly you require a crowd of people
wearing sandals, a cock that crows, a cloak
to dissect, a sponge, some vinegar and one
man to hammer the nails home.

Or you can take a length of steel,
shaped and chased in a traditional way,
and attempt to pierce the metal cage he wears.
But for this you need white horses,
English trees, men with bows and arrows,
at least two flags, a prince and a
castle to hold your banquet in.

Dispensing with nobility, you may, if the wind
allows, blow gas at him. But then you need
a mile of mud sliced through with ditches,
not to mention black boots, bomb craters,
more mud, a plague of rats, a dozen songs
and some round hats made of steel.

In an age of aeroplanes, you may fly
miles above your victim and dispose of him by
pressing one small switch. All you then
require is an ocean to separate you, two
systems of government, a nation's scientists,
several factories, a psychopath and
land that no one needs for several years.

These are, as I began, cumbersome ways
to kill a man. Simpler, direct, and much more neat
is to see that he is living somewhere in the middle
of the twentieth century, and leave him there.

EDWIN BROCK

RUPERT BROOKE (1887-1915): *Son of a housemaster at England's famous Rugby School, Brooke showed great vitality in his love of both literature and sports. Popular, handsome, a highly successful student at Cambridge University and an ardent world traveller, his early death in 1915 helped turn him into something of a legend. Immediately volunteering for service at the outbreak of the First World War in 1914, he was sent to the Mediterranean, where he died of sunstroke. His will directed that royalties from his writings be shared between three of his poet friends, including Walter de la Mare.*

The Hill

Breathless, we flung us on the windy hill,
 Laughed in the sun, and kissed the lovely grass.
 You said, "Through glory and ecstasy we pass;
Wind, sun, and earth remain, the birds sing still,
When we are old, are old. . . ."   "And when we die
 All's over that is ours; and life burns on
Through other lovers, other lips," said I,
 – "Heart of my heart, our heaven is now, is won!"
"We are Earth's best, that learnt her lesson here.
 Life is our cry.   We have kept the faith!" we said;
 "We shall go down with unreluctant tread
Rose-crowned into the darkness!" . . . Proud we were,
And laughed, that had such brave true things to say.
 – And then you suddenly cried, and turned away.

RUPERT BROOKE

The Soldier

If I should die, think only this of me:
  That there's some corner of a foreign field
That is for ever England. There shall be
  In that rich earth a richer dust concealed;
A dust whom England bore, shaped, made aware,
  Gave, once, her flowers to love, her ways to roam,
A body of England's, breathing English air,
  Washed by the rivers, blest by suns of home.

And think, this heart, all evil shed away,
  A pulse in the eternal mind, no less
    Gives somewhere back the thoughts by England given;
Her sights and sounds; dreams happy as her day;
  And laughter, learnt of friends; and gentleness,
    In hearts at peace, under an English heaven.

RUPERT BROOKE

In Former Days

In former days we'd both agree
That you were me, and I was you.
What has now happened to us two,
That you are you, and I am me?

BHARTYHARI
TRANSLATED FROM THE SANSKRIT
BY JOHN BROUGH

Song from "Pippa Passes"

The year's at the spring,
And day's at the morn;
Morning's at seven;
The hill-side's dew-pearled;
The lark's on the wing;
The snail's on the thorn;
God's in His Heaven –
All's right with the world!

ROBERT BROWNING
(1812-1889)

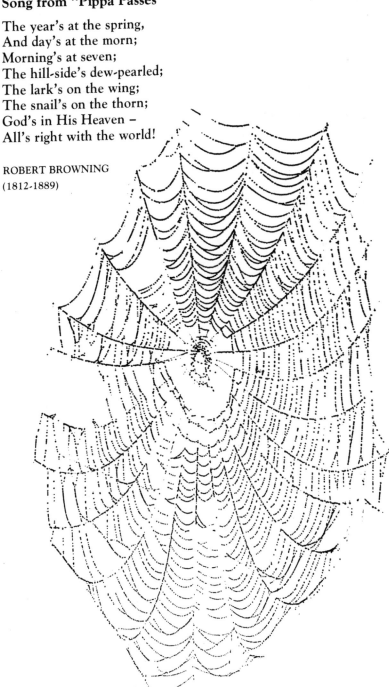

ROBERT BURNS (1757-1796) was the son of a cottar (a peasant who rents a cottage in return for his labour), educated by his father. He is traditionally thought of as Scotland's greatest poet. His best work was produced while he worked as a farmer from 1784 to 1788. In 1786 he published his early poems, and the resulting fame took him to Edinburgh where he became a social and literary sensation. He married Jean Armour, one of his many loves, and returned to farming. His last years he spent as a tax collector, writing little.

A Red, Red Rose

Oh my luve is like a red, red rose,
    That's newly sprung in June;
Oh my luve is like the melodie
    That's sweetly played in tune.

As fair art thou, my bonie lass,
    So deep in luve am I;
And I will luve thee still, my dear,
    Till a' the seas gang dry.

Till a' the seas gang dry, my dear,
    And the rocks melt wi' the sun;
And I will luve thee still, my dear,
    While the sands o' life shall run.

And fare thee weel, my only luve,
    And fare thee weel a while;
And I will come again, my luve,
    Tho' it were ten thousand mile!

ROBERT BURNS

The Short Night

The short night is through:
  on the hairy caterpillar,
  little beads of dew.

TANIGUCHI BUSON (1715-1783)

The Sudden Chillness

The piercing chill I feel:
  my dead wife's comb, in our bedroom,
  under my heel. . . .

TANIGUCHI BUSON

THOMAS CAMPBELL (1777-1844) was the son of a Scottish merchant. He studied law at Glasgow University and wrote on a number of contemporary issues, including the French Revolution and the African slave trade. He is remembered mainly for his rousing war songs. Lord Ullin's Daughter, *like many ballads, has been set to music.*

Lord Ullin's Daughter

A Chieftain to the Highlands bound
   Cries 'Boatman, do not tarry!
And I'll give thee a silver pound
   To row us o'er the ferry!'

'Now who be ye, would cross Lochgyle
   This dark and stormy water?'
'O I'm the chief of Ulva's isle,
   And this, Lord Ullin's daughter.

'And fast before her father's men
   Three days we've fled together,
For should he find us in the glen,
   My blood would stain the heather.

'His horsemen hard behind us ride –
   Should they our steps discover,
Then who will cheer my bonny bride
   When they have slain her lover?'

Out spoke the hardy Highland wight,
   'I'll go, my chief, I'm ready:
It is not for your silver bright,
   But for your winsome lady: –

'And by my word! the bonny bird
   In danger shall not tarry;
So though the waves are raging white
   I'll row you o'er the ferry.'

By this the storm grew loud apace,
   The water-wraith was shrieking;
And in the scowl of heaven each face
   Grew dark as they were speaking.

But still as wilder blew the wind
　　And as the night grew drearer,
Adown the glen rode armèd men,
　　Their trampling sounded nearer.

'O haste thee, haste!' the lady cries,
　　'Though tempests round us gather;
I'll meet the raging of the skies,
　　But not an angry father.'

The boat has left a stormy land,
　　A stormy sea before her, –
When, oh! too strong for human hand
　　The tempest gather'd o'er her.

And still they row'd amidst the roar
　　Of waters fast prevailing:
Lord Ullin reach'd that fatal shore, –
　　His wrath was changed to wailing.

For, sore dismay'd, through storm and shade
　　His child he did discover: –
One lovely hand she stretch'd for aid,
　　And one was round her lover.

'Come back! come back!' he cried in grief
　　'Across this stormy water:
And I'll forgive your Highland chief,
　　My daughter! – O my daughter!'

'Twas vain: the loud waves lash'd the shore,
　　Return or aid preventing:
The waters wild went o'er his child,
　　And he was left lamenting.

THOMAS CAMPBELL

BLISS CARMAN (1861-1929) was born in Fredericton, New Brunswick, and attended the Universities of New Brunswick, Edinburgh, and Harvard. In 1890 he went to New York to work as a literary journalist, but for most of his life he had neither a regular job nor a permanent home. Much of his poetry is romantic landscape poetry of a sort not very popular today.

A Vagabond Song

There is something in the autumn that is native to my blood –
Touch of manner, hint of mood;
And my heart is like a rhyme,
With the yellow and the purple and the crimson keeping time.

The scarlet of the maples can shake me like a cry
Of bugles going by.
And my lonely spirit thrills
To see the frosty asters like a smoke upon the hills.

There is something in October sets the gypsy blood astir;
We must rise and follow her,
When from every hill of flame
She calls and calls each vagabond by name.

BLISS CARMAN

G.K. CHESTERTON (1874-1936): Born in London, England, Chesterton achieved no great distinction at school or university, being known as a rather sleepy student showing occasional excellence. Contacts in the publishing world started him on what turned out to be a brilliant literary and journalistic career. Dominating his writing is his religious view of the world. He once said, "I am quite incapable of talking or writing about Dutch gardens or the game of chess, but if I did, I have no doubt that what I would say or write about them would be coloured by my view of the cosmos."

The Donkey

When fishes flew and forests walked
    And figs grew upon thorn,
Some moment when the moon was blood
    Then surely I was born;

With monstrous head and sickening cry
    And ears like errant wings,

   The devil's walking parody
      On all four-footed things.

   The tattered outlaw of the earth,
      Of ancient crooked will;
Starve, scourge, deride me: I am dumb,
    I keep my secret still.

Fools! For I also had my hour;
    One far fierce hour and sweet:
There was a shout about my ears,
    And palms before my feet.

G. K. CHESTERTON

*LEONARD COHEN (1934-   ) was born in Montreal and
attended McGill and Columbia Universities. Poet, novelist,
songwriter and singer, he performed in Montreal nightclubs
and later for the CBC. "We are on the threshold of a great
religious age," Cohen has said, and his idea of the poet's
function seems similar to that of the priest's function –
awakening people to what is beautiful and holy within them-
selves and within the universe. He is able to do this without
sentimentalism.*

The Bus

I was the last passenger of the day,
I was alone on the bus,
I was glad they were spending all that money
just getting me up Eighth Avenue.
Driver! I shouted, it's you and me tonight,
let's run away from this big city
to a smaller city more suitable to the heart,
let's drive past the swimming pools of Miami Beach,
you in the driver's seat, me several seats back,
but in the racial cities we'll change places
so as to show how well you've done up North,
and let us find ourselves some tiny American fishing village
in unknown Florida
and park right at the edge of the sand,
a huge bus pointing out,
metallic, painted, solitary,
with New York plates.

LEONARD COHEN

For Anne

With Annie gone,
Whose eyes to compare
With the morning sun?

Not that I did compare,
But I do compare
Now that she's gone.

LEONARD COHEN

Epigram

Sir, I admit your general rule,
That every poet is a fool,
But you yourself may serve to show it,
That every fool is not a poet.

SAMUEL TAYLOR COLERIDGE (1772-1834)

FRANCES CORNFORD (1886-1960) was a granddaughter of Charles Darwin and married to the English philosopher Francis Cornford. She lived in Cambridge, where she befriended many young poets, including Rupert Brooke.

To a Fat Lady Seen from the Train

O why do you walk through the fields in gloves,
   Missing so much and so much?
O fat white woman whom nobody loves,
Why do you walk through the fields in gloves,
When the grass is soft as the breast of doves
   And shivering-sweet to the touch?
O why do you walk through the fields in gloves,
   Missing so much and so much?

FRANCES CORNFORD

For a Father

With the exact length and pace of his father's stride
The son walks,
Echoes and intonations of his father's speech
Are heard when he talks.

Once when the table was tall,
And the chair a wood,
He absorbed his father's smile and carefully copied
The way that he stood.

He grew into exile slowly,
With pride and remorse,
In some ways better than his begetters,
In others worse.

And now having chosen, with strangers,
Half glad of his choice,
He smiles with his father's hesitant smile
And speaks with his voice.

ANTHONY CRONIN (1925-   )

CHIEF CROWFOOT (1830?-1890) was a Blackfoot Indian who, although he was known as a fine scout and a warrior, discouraged attacks on the whites. In 1866 he rescued a white priest from a band of hostile Crees. He cooperated with the whites by restraining his warriors when the Canadian Pacific Railway went through their lands in 1884, but he was unable to prevent the demoralization of his people by the whisky dealers.

Farewell

A little while
and
I will be gone from among you,
whither I cannot tell.
From nowhere we come;
into nowhere we go.

What is life?
It is a flash of a firefly
in the night.
It is a breath of a buffalo
in the winter time.
It is the little shadow
that runs across the grass
and loses itself in the sunset.

CROWFOOT, BLACKFOOT CHIEF,
HIS DYING WORDS.

E.E. CUMMINGS (1894-1962): Born in Massachusetts, cummings graduated from Harvard, served in the First World War and studied art in Paris. He finally settled in New Hampshire with his wife, where he wrote and painted. His poetry shows humour and delight in physical pleasures and heartfelt emotion. The experimental nature of his poetry, especially the way it looks, has attracted a lot of controversy and has certainly been a liberating force in modern poetry.

in Just–spring

in Just –
spring   when the world is mud-
luscious the little
lame balloonman

whistles   far   and wee

and eddieandbill come
running from marbles and
piracies and it's
spring

when the world is puddle-wonderful

the queer
old balloonman whistles
far   and   wee
and bettyandisabel come dancing

from hop-scotch and jump-rope and

it's
spring
and

    the

        goat-footed

balloonMan   whistles
far
and
wee

e.e. cummings

ROBERT CURRIE (1937-   ) is a Canadian poet who lives with his wife and two children in Moose Jaw, Saskatchewan, where he teaches English at Central Collegiate. Of his first published collection of poems, Diving Into Fire, *one critic said, ". . . his poems are not passing thoughts or fanciful fits of passion. They are the substance of life that has been lived and loved, enjoyed and endured."*

The Test
For Jim McLean

The boy was ten years old
and the BB gun almost as big as he
He'd wandered far that day
potting at gophers and clumps of dirt
Going back to town
his legs were dragging
as if they wanted to lie down
and let him go on alone
He sought the CP tracks
as the quickest way home
but when he came to the bridge
that rode over the sleepy creek
he knew it was time to rest
He found the tie hard on his rear
and slipped off it to the grass
that ran greenly down the bank
He lay wriggling his toes in his sneakers
feeling like a man after a hard day's work
He must have dozed off
until the whistle shrilled in the distance
He sat up and down the line
the train was steaming at him
He felt an idea stir within
and edged nearer the tracks
There was nobody to prove a thing to
and only him to see
And what you did alone meant more
He folded his arms across his chest
and waited.

Again the whistle blew
The rails now were humming beside him
and he could sense the engine's breath upon him
He closed his eyes
and thrust himself against the tie
The whistle shrieked for him to move
but he held firm
Just as the engine hurled toward him
he knew that he must see it come
He looked up locking eyes with the engineer
and reading the curse that he couldn't hear
Then the steam and the driving wheels
He pressed against the tie
leaning into the fear
that pushed him away
The boxcars washed by him
and soon the red of caboose
      and he hadn't moved
As the clanking died
he smiled down the miles of empty track
and swung onto new legs
that beat out his victory march
along the ties to town.

ROBERT CURRIE

*ROY DANIELLS (1902-): Born in England, Daniells
emigrated to Canada with his family when he was eight.
He followed a university teaching career, becoming Head of
the English department at the University of British Columbia.
Most of his poems are sonnets. He has said that the strongest
influences on his writing have been religion, Canadian
history, and travel in Europe.*

All Through the 'Thirties

All through the 'thirties, south of Saskatoon,
A farmer farmed a farm without a crop.
Dust filled the air, the lamp was lit at noon,
And never blade of wheat that formed a top.
One New Year's to the hired man he said,
'I have no money. You must take the deeds.
And I will be the hired man instead,
To shovel snow and fork the tumbleweeds.'
So it was done. And when the next year came,
'Take back the farm,' the other had to say.
And year by year, alternate, just the same
Till the War came and took them both away.
With such superb resource and self-possession
Canada made it through the long depression.

ROY DANIELLS

W.H. DAVIES (1871-1940): *Born in Wales, the son of a publican, Davies had little formal education. At age twenty-two he set out for a vagrant life in North America where he begged and did casual labour well into his thirties. Train-jumping to get around, he lost his right leg below the knee while trying to get from Renfrew, Ontario, to the Klondike. He returned to London, England, where his* Autobiography of a Super-Tramp *(1907) brought him much publicity. He continued to write, and gained wide acclaim, until his death at age sixty-nine.*

Leisure

What is this life if, full of care,
We have no time to stand and stare.

No time to stand beneath the boughs
And stare as long as sheep or cows.

No time to see, when woods we pass,
Where squirrels hide their nuts in grass.

No time to see, in broad daylight,
Streams full of stars, like skies at night.

No time to turn at Beauty's glance,
And watch her feet, how they can dance.

No time to wait till her mouth can
Enrich that smile her eyes began.

A poor life this if, full of care,
We have no time to stand and stare.

W.H. DAVIES

WALTER DE LA MARE (1873-1956) was born in England. His formal education ended when he was seventeen, when, with his long wavy hair and his velvet coat, he took up work as a bookkeeper for an oil company. But his literary talents were soon recognized, eventually providing him and his family with a secure living. In his interest in the borderline between the "real" and the "unreal," de la Mare once said that "our one hope is to get away from realism, in the accepted sense. An imaginative experience is not only as real but far realer than an unimaginative one."

in forest (tower, turret) big
can't be small, empty, echos

The Listeners

"Is there anybody there?" said the Traveller,
   Knocking on the moonlit door:
And his horse in the silence champed the grasses
   Of the forest's ferny floor:
And a bird flew up out of the turret,
   Above the Traveller's head:
And he smote upon the door again a second time:
   "Is there anybody there?" he said.
But no one descended to the Traveller;
   No head from the leaf-fringed sill
Leaned over and looked into his grey eyes,
   Where he stood perplexed and still.
But only a host of phantom listeners
   That dwelt in the lone house then
Stood listening in the quiet of the moonlight
   To that voice from the world of men:
Stood thronging the faint moonbeams on the dark stair,
   That goes down to the empty hall,
Hearkening in an air stirred and shaken
   By the lonely Traveller's call.
And he felt in his heart their strangeness,
   Their stillness answering his cry,
While his horse moved, cropping the dark turf,
   'Neath the starred and leafy sky;
For he suddenly smote on the door, even
   Louder, and lifted his head: –

"Tell them I came, and no one answered,
  That I kept my word," he said.
Never the least stir made the listeners,
  Though every word he spake
Fell echoing through the shadowiness of the still house
  From the one man left awake:
Ay, they heard his foot upon the stirrup,
  And the sound of iron on stone
And how the silence surged softly backward,
  When the plunging hoofs were gone.

WALTER DE LA MARE

Scholars

    Logic does well at school;
And Reason answers every question right;
Poll-parrot Memory unwinds her spool;
And Copy-cat keeps Teacher well in sight:

The Heart's a truant; nothing does by rule;
Safe in its wisdom, is taken for a fool;
Nods through the morning on the dunce's stool;
    And wakes to dream all night.

WALTER DE LA MARE

EMILY DICKINSON (1830-1886): *Born in Amherst, Massachusetts, she spent almost all her life in the same house and garden. She was an eccentric and an extreme individualist; the reason for her withdrawal from the world is unknown. She wore only white, avoided visitors, and had two great passions – her garden and her poetry. Only five of her poems were published in her lifetime. She wrote over a thousand. It is due to her sister Lavinia, who found the hoard of poems on odd scraps of paper after Emily's death, that these too were eventually made public.*

Apparently with No Surprise

Apparently with no surprise
To any happy flower,
The frost beheads it at its play
In accidental power.

The blond assassin passes on,
The sun proceeds unmoved
To measure off another day
For an approving God.

EMILY DICKINSON

Chartless

I never saw a moor,
I never saw the sea;
Yet know I how the heather looks,
And what a wave must be.

I never spoke with God,
Nor visited in heaven;
Yet certain am I of the spot
As if the chart were given.

EMILY DICKINSON

The Train

I like to see it lap the miles,
And lick the valleys up,
And stop to feed itself at tanks;
And then, prodigious, step

Around a pile of mountains,
And, supercilious, peer
In shanties by the sides of roads;
And then a quarry pare

To fit its sides, and crawl between,
Complaining all the while
In horrid, hooting stanza;
Then chase itself down hill

And neigh like Boanerges;
Then, punctual as a star,
Stop – docile and omnipotent –
At its own stable door.

EMILY DICKINSON

New Hampshire

Children's voices in the orchard
Between the blossom- and the fruit-time:
Golden head, crimson head,
Between the green tip and the root.
Black wing, brown wing, hover over;
Twenty years and the spring is over;
To-day grieves, to-morrow grieves,
Cover me over, light-in-leaves;
Golden head, black wing,
Cling, swing,
Spring, sing,
Swing up into the apple-tree.

T.S. ELIOT

T.S. ELIOT (1888-1965): American-born, Eliot became a British
subject in 1927. Educated at Oxford, he was an admirer
of tradition in literature, politics and religion, but he was
far from traditional in his poetry. He is usually thought of
as "difficult" because of his wide use of symbolism and the
"stream of thought" nature of his poetry.

The Cyclist

Back bent; hands gripped; breath coming heavily;
face flushed; brow damp; feet driving steadily;
teeth clenched; lips wide; chain grinding rustily.
Lord! what a hill! Breeze blowing gustily.

Now for the top! Just-a few-yards-away.
Drive-down-the-pedals – hard!   hard! – We're up!
    hooray!
Poised here an instant – downhill before us –
now hear the wheels sing crescendo in chorus,

down, down the long, falling roadway flushed and
    radiant-
ly fast-and-faster, fast-and-faster whining down the
    gradient
with tyres a slur-and-slither and the spokes like
    organs droning
to the long, smooth, straight, spread road slow
    homing.

ROBERT FARREN (1909-   )

75

KENNETH FEARING (1902-1961): *Born in Illinois, Fearing worked as a reporter, a salesman, mill-hand, and clerk. He became a poet of the proletariat. "I will suffer fools, though not gladly," he said, "but I can't endure stuffed shirts." Political convictions were a mystery to him, and his favourite writers were those who did not "pretend to know more about life than the rest of us . . ."*

Confession Overheard in a Subway

You will ask how I came to be eavesdropping, in the
    first place.
The answer is, I was not.
The man who confessed to these several crimes (call
    him John Doe) spoke into my right ear on a
    crowded subway train, while the man whom he ad-
    dressed (call him Richard Roe) stood at my left.
Thus, I stood between them, and they talked, or some-
    times shouted, quite literally straight through me.
How could I help but overhear?
Perhaps I might have moved away to some other strap.
    But the aisles were full.
Besides, I felt, for some reason, curious.

"I do not deny my guilt," said John Doe. "My own, first,
    and after that my guilty knowledge of still further
    guilt.
I have counterfeited often, and successfully.
I have been guilty of ignorance, and talking with con-
    viction. Of intolerable wisdom, and keeping silent.
Through carelessness, or cowardice, I have shortened
    the lives of better men. And the name for that is
    murder.
All my life I have been a receiver of stolen goods."
"Personally, I always mind my own business," said
    Richard Roe. "Sensible people don't get into those
    scrapes."

I was not the only one who overheard this confession.

Several businessmen, bound for home, and housewives and mechanics, were within easy earshot.

A policeman sitting in front of us did not lift his eyes, at the mention of murder, from his paper.

Why should I be the one to report these crimes?

You will understand why this letter to your paper is anonymous. I will sign it: Public Spirited Citizen, and hope that it cannot be traced.

But all the evidence, if there is any clamor for it, can be substantiated.

I have heard the same confession many times since, in different places.

And now that I think of it, I had heard it many times before.

"Guilt," said John, "is always and everywhere nothing less than guilt.

I have always, at all times, been a willing accomplice of the crass and the crude.

I have overheard, daily, the smallest details of con-spiracies against the human race, vast in their ulti-mate scope, and conspired, daily, to launch my own.

You have heard of innocent men who died in the chair. It was my greed that threw the switch.

I helped, and I do not deny it, to nail that guy to the cross, and shall continue to help.

Look into my eyes, you can see the guilt.

Look at my face, my hair, my very clothing, you will see guilt written plainly everywhere.

Guilt of the flesh. Of the soul. Of laughing, when others do not. Of breathing and eating and sleeping.

I am guilty of what? Of guilt. Guilty of guilt, that is all, and enough."

Richard Roe looked at his wristwatch and said: "We'll be twenty minutes late.

After dinner we might take in a show."

Now, who will bring John Doe to justice for his measure-less crimes?

I do not, personally, wish to be involved.
Such nakedness of the soul belongs in some other prov-
    ince, probably the executioner's.
And who will bring the blunt and upright Richard Roe
    to the accuser's stand, where he belongs?
Or will he deny and deny his partnership?

I have done my duty, as a public spirited citizen, in any
    case.

KENNETH FEARING

LAWRENCE FERLINGHETTI (1919-   ): Born in New York, he now works as a publisher and writer in San Francisco, where he has encouraged and published numerous young authors. One of the founders of the Beat group of poets, he believes (as did Walt Whitman) that the poet should be an agitator whose messages should reach the greater mass of people. His poetry shows understanding of the spiritual side of humanity, and intense moral concern over the materialism of society.

Constantly risking absurdity and death

        Constantly risking absurdity
                              and death
                whenever he performs
                              above the heads
                                    of his audience
         the poet like an acrobat
                        climbs on rime
                              to a high wire of his own making
and balancing on eyebeams
                              above a sea of faces
                paces his way
                        to the other side of day
            performing entrechats
                              and sleight-of-foot tricks
and other high theatrics
                        and all without mistaking
                any thing
                        for what it may not be

         For he's the super realist
                              who must perforce perceive
                taut truth
                        before the taking of each stance or step
    in his supposed advance
                              toward that still higher perch
    where Beauty stands and waits
                        with gravity
                              to start her death-defying leap

         And he
                a little charleychaplin man
                              who may or may not catch
                her fair eternal form
                              spreadeagled in the empty air
                    of existence

LAWRENCE FERLINGHETTI

JAMES ELROY FLECKER (1884-1915) was an English poet
and playwright. As a child he was highly-strung, clever, and
quarrelsome. He began writing verse at age thirteen.
He attended both Oxford and Cambridge universities, joined
the consular service, and married a Greek woman. The last
five years of his life were spent in and out of hospitals.
He died at thirty of tuberculosis.

To a Poet a Thousand Years Hence

I who am dead a thousand years,
    And wrote this sweet archaic song,
Send you my words for messengers
    The way I shall not pass along.

I care not if you bridge the seas,
    Or ride secure the cruel sky,
Or build consummate palaces
    Of metal or of masonry.

But have you wine and music still,
    And statues and a bright-eyed love,
And foolish thoughts of good and ill,
    And prayers to them who sit above?

How shall we conquer? Like a wind
    That falls at eve our fancies blow,
And old Mæonides the blind
    Said it three thousand years ago.

O friend unseen, unborn, unknown,
    Student of our sweet English tongue,
Read out my words at night, alone:
    I was a poet, I was young.

Since I can never see your face,
    And never shake you by the hand,
I send my soul through time and space
    To greet you. You will understand.

JAMES ELROY FLECKER

ROBERT FROST (1874-1963) was born in New England, where his first attempts at making a living as a poet went unrewarded. Encouraged by his wife, he sold their farm in 1912 and went to England, where he had two books of poetry published in two years. They were republished in the U.S.A., and Frost and his family were soon settled again on a New Hampshire farm. He continued to write successfully, mainly about the life and people of New England. Of poetry he once said, "[it] makes you remember what you didn't know you knew."

The Runaway

Once when the snow of the year was beginning to fall,
We stopped by a mountain pasture to say, "Whose colt?"
A little Morgan had one forefoot on the wall,
The other curled at his breast. He dipped his head
And snorted to us. And then he had to bolt.
We heard the miniature thunder where he fled,
And we saw him, or thought we saw him, dim and gray,
Like a shadow against the curtain of falling flakes.
"I think the little fellow's afraid of the snow.
He isn't winter-broken. It isn't play
With the little fellow at all. He's running away.
I doubt if even his mother could tell him, 'Sakes,
It's only weather.' He'd think she didn't know!
Where is his mother? He can't be out alone."
And now he comes again with a clatter of stone
And mounts the wall again with whited eyes
And all his tail that isn't hair up straight.
He shudders his coat as if to throw off flies.
"Whoever it is that leaves him out so late,
When other creatures have gone to stall and bin,
Ought to be told to come and take him in."

ROBERT FROST

The Span of Life

The old dog barks backward without getting up.
I can remember when he was a pup.

ROBERT FROST

ZONA GALE (1874-1938) was an American writer whose first "book" was printed and bound by herself at the age of seven. She wrote ceaselessly, became famous and prosperous, adopted two little girls, and married, at age fifty-four, a man she had known since childhood.

North Star

His boy had stolen some money from a booth
At the County Fair. I found the father in his kitchen.
For years he had driven a dray and the heavy lifting
Had worn him down. So through his evenings
He slept by the kitchen stove as I found him.
The mother was crying and ironing.
I thought about the mother,
For she brought me a photograph
Taken at a street fair on her wedding day.
She was so trim and white and he so neat and alert.
In the picture with their friends about them –
I saw that she wanted me to know their dignity from the first.
But afterward I thought more about the father.
For as he came with me to the door
I could not forbear to say how bright and near the stars seemed.
Then he leaned and peered from beneath his low roof
And he said:
"There used to be a star called the Nord Star."

ZONA GALE

I Have Known You, from <u>My Heart Soars</u>

I have known you
when your forests were mine;
when they gave me my meat
and clothing.
I have known you
in your streams
and rivers
where your fish flashed
and danced in the sun,
where the waters said come,
come and eat of my abundance.
I have known you
in the freedom of your winds.
And my spirit,
like the winds,
once roamed your good lands.

For thousands of years
I have spoken the language of the land
and listened to its many voices.
I took what I needed
and found there was plenty for everyone.
The rivers were clear and thick with life,
the air was pure and gave way
to the thrashing of countless wings.
On land, a profusion of creatures abounded.

83

I walked tall and proud
knowing the resourcefulness of my people,
feeling the blessings of the Supreme Spirit.
I lived in the brotherhood of all beings.
I measured the day
by the sun's journey across the sky.
The passing of the year was told
by the return of the salmon
or the birds pairing off to nest.
Between the first campfire and the last
of each day I searched for food,
made shelter, clothing and weapons,
and always found time for prayer.

The wisdom and eloquence of my father
I passed on to my children,
so they too acquired faith,
courage, generosity, understanding,
and knowledge in the proper way of living.
Such are the memories of yesterday!
Today, harmony still lives in nature,
though we have less wilderness,
less variety of creatures.
Fewer people know the cougar's den
in the hills, nor have their eyes followed
the eagle's swoop, as he writes endless
circles into the warm air.

The wild beauty of the coastline
and the taste of sea fog remains hidden
behind the windows of passing cars.
When the last bear's skin has been taken
and the last ram's head has been mounted
and fitted with glass eyes,
we may find in them the reflection
of today's memories.
Take care, or soon our ears will strain
in vain to hear the creator's song.

CHIEF DAN GEORGE

SIR WILLIAM S. GILBERT (1836-1911) was a British writer who, after serving in the militia and working as a clerk, began his literary career in 1861 as a contributor to Fun *magazine. Well-known as a writer of humorous verse, he achieved lasting fame when he began working with the composer Sir Arthur Sullivan on a long series of comic operas (the Gilbert and Sullivan operas), including* The Pirates of Penzance *and* H.M.S. Pinafore.

Nightmare

When you're lying awake with a dismal headache, and
    repose is taboo'd by anxiety,
I conceive you may use any language you choose to
    indulge in, without impropriety;
For your brain is on fire – the bedclothes conspire of
    usual slumber to plunder you:
First your counterpane goes, and uncovers your toes,
    and your sheet slips demurely from under you;
Then the blanketing tickles – you feel like mixed pickles –
    so terribly sharp is the pricking,
And you're hot, and you're cross, and you tumble and
    toss till there's nothing 'twixt you and the ticking.
Then the bedclothes all creep to the ground in a heap,
    and you pick 'em all up in a tangle;
Next your pillow resigns and politely declines to remain
    at its usual angle!
Well, you get some repose in the form of a doze, with
    hot eye-balls and head ever aching,
But your slumbering teems with such horrible dreams
    that you'd very much better be waking;
For you dream you are crossing the Channel, and tossing
    about in a steamer from Harwich –
Which is something between a large bathing machine
    and a very small second-class carriage –
And you're giving a treat (penny ice and cold meat) to
    a party of friends and relations –
They're a ravenous horde – and they all came on board
    at Sloane Square and South Kensington Stations.
And bound on that journey you find your attorney (who
    started that morning from Devon);
He's a bit undersized, and you don't feel surprised when
    he tells you he's only eleven.

Well, you're driving like mad with this singular lad
    (by-the-bye the ship's now a four-wheeler),
And you're playing round games, and he calls you bad
    names when you tell him that 'ties pay the dealer';
But this you can't stand, so you throw up your hand, and
    you find you're as cold as an icicle,
In your shirt and your socks (the black silk with gold
    clocks), crossing Salisbury Plain on a bicycle:
And he and the crew are on bicycles too – which they've
    somehow or other invested in –
And he's telling the tars, all the particu*lars* of a company
    he's interested in –
It's a scheme of devices, to get at low prices, all goods
    from cough mixtures to cables
(Which tickled the sailors) by treating retailers, as
    though they were all vege*ta*bles –
You get a good spadesman to plant a small tradesman,
    (first take off his boots with a boot-tree),
And his legs will take root, and his fingers will shoot,
    and they'll blossom and bud like a fruit-tree –
From the greengrocer tree you get grapes and green pea,
    cauliflower, pineapple, and cranberries,
While the pastrycook plant, cherry brandy will grant,
    apple puffs, and three-corners, and banberries –
The shares are a penny, and ever so many are taken by
    Rothschild and Baring,
And just as a few are allotted to you, you awake with a
    shudder despairing –
You're a regular wreck, with a crick in your neck, and
    no wonder you snore, for your head's on the floor,
    and you've needles and pins from your soles to your
    shins, and your flesh is a-creep for your left leg's
    asleep, and you've cramp in your toes, and a fly on
    your nose, and some fluff in your lung, and a
    feverish tongue, and a thirst that's intense, and a
    general sense that you haven't been sleeping in
    clover;
But the darkness has passed, and it's daylight at last,
    and the night has been long – ditto ditto my song –
    and thank goodness they're both of them over!

W.S. GILBERT

*OLIVER GOLDSMITH (1728-1774), the son of an Irish clergy-
man, was light-hearted, whimsical, and somewhat irrespon-
sible. He studied medicine at Edinburgh, and eventually
attained a medical degree at a foreign university during his
wanderings through France, Switzerland and Italy. He arrived
in London destitute in 1756, where he earned a meagre living
as a physician, usher, and a hack writer, while he wrote a
great deal. His good friend Samuel Johnson saved him from
arrest for debt by selling his novel* The Vicar of Wakefield
for him.

Elegy on the Death of a Mad Dog

Good people all, of every sort,
   Give ear unto my song;
And if you find it wond'rous short,
   It cannot hold you long.

In Islington there was a man,
   Of whom the world might say,
That still a godly race he ran,
   Whene'er he went to pray.

A kind and gentle heart he had,
   To comfort friends and foes;
The naked every day he clad,
   When he put on his clothes.

And in that town a dog was found,
   As many dogs there be,
Both mongrel, puppy, whelp, and hound,
   And curs of low degree.

This dog and man at first were friends;
   But when a pique began,
The dog, to gain some private ends,
   Went mad and bit the man.

Around from all the neighbouring streets
   The wond'ring neighbours ran,

And swore the dog had lost its wits,
  To bite so good a man.

The wound it seem'd both sore and sad
  To every Christian eye;
And while they swore the dog was mad,
  They swore the man would die.

But soon a wonder came to light,
  That showed the rogues they lied:
The man recover'd of the bite,
  The dog it was that died.

OLIVER GOLDSMITH

GERALD GOULD (1885-1936) was an English journalist, poet, and literary critic. He attended London and Oxford Universities. He is remembered chiefly for the poem that appears here.

Wander-Thirst

Beyond the East the sunrise, beyond the West
    the sea,
And East and West the wander-thirst that will not
    let me be;
It works in me like madness, dear, to bid me say
    good-bye;
For the seas call and the stars call, and oh! the
    call of the sky.

I know not where the white road runs, nor what
    the blue hills are,
But a man can have the sun for friend, and for his
    guide a star;
And there's no end of voyaging when once the
    voice is heard,
For the rivers call and the roads call, and oh!
    the call of a bird!

Yonder the long horizon lies, and there by night
    and day
The old ships draw to home again, the young
    ships sail away;
And come I may, but go I must, and, if men ask
    you why,
You may put the blame on the stars and the Sun
    and the white road and the sky.

GERALD GOULD

ROBERT GRAVES (1895-   ): *Born in England, Graves went directly from school into the First World War. Apart from two university professorships, he earned his living by writing – novels, an auto-biography, translations, essays and poetry. Unlike many other moderns, he is not so much interested in the physical form of poetry but in originality of thought and image. He seems to draw upon a hidden reservoir of human knowledge and images –* Warning to Children *has the unusual psychological impact typical of Graves.*

Flying Crooked

The butterfly, the cabbage-white,
(His honest idiocy of flight)
Will never now, it is too late,
Master the art of flying straight,
Yet has – who knows so well as I? –
A just sense of how not to fly:
He lurches here and here by guess
And God and hope and hopelessness.
Even the aerobatic swift
Has not his flying-crooked gift.

ROBERT GRAVES

Warning to Children

Children, if you dare to think
Of the greatness, rareness, muchness,
Fewness of this precious only
Endless world in which you say
You live, you think of things like this:
Blocks of slate enclosing dappled
Red and green, enclosing tawny
Yellow nets, enclosing white
And black acres of dominoes,
Where a neat brown paper parcel
Tempts you to untie the string.
In the parcel a small island,
On the island a large tree,
On the tree a husky fruit.
Strip the husk and pare the rind off:
In the kernel you will see
Blocks of slate enclosed by dappled
Red and green, enclosed by tawny
Yellow nets, enclosed by white
And black acres of dominoes,
Where the same brown paper parcel –
Children, leave the string alone!
For who dares undo the parcel
Finds himself at once inside it,
On the island, in the fruit,
Blocks of slate about his head,
Finds himself enclosed by dappled
Green and red, enclosed by yellow
Tawny nets, enclosed by black
And white acres of dominoes,
With the same brown paper parcel
Still untied upon his knee.
And, if he then should dare to think
Of the fewness, muchness, rareness,
Greatness of this endless only
Precious world in which he says
He lives – he then unties the string.

ROBERT GRAVES

ELDON GRIER (1917-   ) was born in England of Canadian parents and raised in Montreal. He turned to poetry at age thirty-five after many years as a painter. His poems have appeared both in Canadian magazines and international collections.

Bury Me in My Cadillac

Perfectly grooved
with God, of course,
as my quarterback,
I've breached the hillside of success,
the solidly tricked suburbia;
raked the ceremonial leaves,
fringed my famished fancy
with a flower bed.
Vested in perma-stone,
I cannot now turn back.
Geronimo!

ELDON GRIER

ARTHUR GUITERMAN (1871-1943) was an American who, after attending the College of the City of New York, worked as a reporter and editor before becoming a freelance writer. He wrote some serious poetry, but is best known for his light verse. Because his name was often mispronounced, a friend wrote this helpful couplet for him:
There ain't no better, fitter man
Than Mister Arthur Guiterman.

On the Vanity of Earthly Greatness

The tusks that clashed in mighty brawls
Of mastodons, are billiard balls.

The sword of Charlemagne the Just
Is ferric oxide, known as rust.

The grizzly bear whose potent hug
Was feared by all, is now a rug.

Great Caesar's dead and on the shelf,
And I don't feel so well myself!

ARTHUR GUITERMAN

Fueled

Fueled
by a million
man-made
wings of fire –
the rocket tore a tunnel
through the sky –
and everybody cheered.
Fueled
only by a thought from God –
the seedling
urged its way
through the thicknesses of black –
and as it pierced
the heavy ceiling of the soil –
and launched itself
up into outer space –
no
one
even
clapped.

MARCIE HANS

THOMAS HARDY (1840-1928) was an English novelist whose
novels reflected such pessimism over humanity's struggle
against "indifferent" fate that the general outcry against
them drove him to abandon the novel altogether – he wrote
only poetry for the last thirty years of his life. Much of his
poetry, too, reflects his pessimism, yet there was nothing in
his life circumstances to explain this point of view.

Heredity

I am the family face;
Flesh perishes, I live on,
Projecting trait and trace
Through time to times anon,
And leaping from place to place
Over oblivion.

The years-heired feature that can
In curve and voice and eye
Despise the human span
Of durance – that is I;
The eternal thing in man,
That heeds no call to die.

THOMAS HARDY

*WILLIAM ERNEST HENLEY (1849-1903): Born in England,
the son of a bookseller, Henley was crippled from boyhood.
While in hospital from 1873-75 he wrote* Hospital Verses.
*These poems came to the attention of the writer Robert Louis
Stevenson, who visited Henley in hospital. Encouraged,
Henley later did a great deal of literary work apart from
writing poetry, including writing plays in collaboration with
Stevenson, but he is chiefly remembered for the following
poem.*

Unconquerable

Out of the night that covers me,
　　Black as the pit from pole to pole,
I thank whatever gods may be
　　For my unconquerable soul.

In the fell clutch of circumstance
　　I have not winced nor cried aloud.
Under the bludgeonings of chance
　　My head is bloody, but unbow'd.

Beyond this place of wrath and tears
　　Looms but the Horror of the shade,
And yet the menace of the years
　　Finds, and shall find, me unafraid.

It matters not how strait the gate,
　　How charged with punishments the scroll,
I am the master of my fate:
　　I am the captain of my soul.

WILLIAM ERNEST HENLEY

ROBERT HERRICK (1591-1674) was born in London and educated at Cambridge. After spending some time as apprentice to a goldsmith he became a country vicar in Devonshire. He was a great admirer of Ben Jonson.

Upon Julia's Clothes

Whenas in silks my Julia goes,
Then, then, methinks, how sweetly flows
The liquefaction of her clothes.

Next, when I cast mine eyes, and see
That brave vibration, each way free,
Oh, how that glittering taketh me!

ROBERT HERRICK

Sons and Lovers

I do not think that our fathers ever met
But we know from their stories
That their camaraderie was strong.
They slapped backs,
Twisted wrists, shot rabbits,
Fondled rumbleseat girls
Fought Hitler
Thickened their livers with whiskey
And their hands with work
All before they were twenty-five.

We would not have been their comrades
Had we known them then.
What would they have thought
Of spending the whole morning
Watching the eyelids of a sleeping girl
Or leaving half a beer
To go outside and make angels
In the new snow?

RICHARD HORNSEY

*DOM SYLVESTER HOUÉDARD (1924-   ) is a British writer
and Benedictine monk. He is a leading exponent of visual
or "concrete" poetry in England. Western and Eastern
meditation join their influences in his work, which offers no
"literary" elements such as metre or rhyme. His dissolving
of art-categories is regarded with some suspicion as well
as admiration.*

treepoem

how   we   turn   out   to   be   related

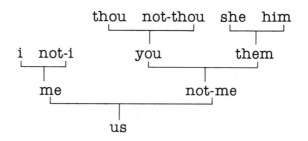

LANGSTON HUGHES (1902-1967), a black American writer, went to high school in Cleveland, where his first poems were published in the school magazine. After working as a trans-Atlantic seaman and a cook in Paris, he worked as a bus boy in a Washington Hotel. There he left three poems beside Vachel Lindsay's plate, which Lindsay later read aloud to the audience in the hotel's theatre. He has since published novels, stories, plays and songs, largely concerned with depicting Negro life in America.

War

The face of war is my face.
The face of war is your face.
   What color
   Is the face
   Of war?
Brown, black, white –
Your face and my face.

Death is the broom
I take in my hands
To sweep the world
   Clean.
I sweep and I sweep
Then mop and I mop.
I dip my broom in blood,
My mop in blood –
And blame you for this,
Because you are *there*,
   Enemy.

It's hard to blame me,
Because I am here –
So I kill you.
And you kill me.
   My name,
Like your name,
   Is war.

LANGSTON HUGHES

Dreams

Hold fast to dreams
For if dreams die
Life is a broken-winged bird
That cannot fly.

Hold fast to dreams
For when dreams go
Life is a barren field
Frozen with snow.

LANGSTON HUGHES

LEIGH HUNT (James Henry Leigh, 1784-1859) was born in England. He edited a magazine called The Examiner *and was sent to jail with his brother, and fined, for publishing certain opinions about the Prince Regent. He continued his editorial duties from jail, where he was visited by several famous writers. He introduced Keats and Shelley to each other, and introduced both to the public in* The Examiner. *He is remembered mainly for his recognition of the genius of these two men and for the development of the light miscellaneous essay.*

Abou Ben Adhem

Abou Ben Adhem – may his tribe increase! –
Awoke one night from a deep dream of peace,
And saw, within the moonlight in his room,
Making it rich and like a lily in bloom,
An angel writing in a book of gold.
Exceeding peace had made Ben Adhem bold,
And to the presence in the room he said:
"What writest thou?"   The vision raised its head,
And with a look made of all sweet accord,
Answered: "The names of those who love the Lord."
"And is mine one?" said Abou.   "Nay not so,"
Replied the angel.   Abou spoke more low,
But cheerily still; and said: "I pray thee, then,
Write me as one that loves his fellow-men."
The angel wrote, and vanished.   The next night
It came again with a great wakening light,
And shewed the names whom love of God had blessed,
And lo! Ben Adhem's name led all the rest.

LEIGH HUNT

Jenny Kiss'd Me

Jenny kiss'd me when we met,
    Jumping from the chair she sat in;
Time, you thief, who love to get
    Sweets into your list, put that in!
Say I'm weary, say I'm sad,
    Say that health and wealth have miss'd me,
Say I'm growing old, but add,
    Jenny kiss'd me.

LEIGH HUNT

Spring

Snow melts,
        and the village is overflowing –
            with the children.

ISSA (1762-1826)

E. PAULINE JOHNSON (1862-1913) was the daughter of a Mohawk chief and an English mother, born on the Six Nations Reserve near Brantford, Ontario, and given a liberal education at home. Her lyrics began to appear in Canadian, American and English magazines in 1885. Her fame increased when she began to make national and international tours, dressed in Indian costume, reciting her poems. In 1909 she retired and went to live in Vancouver, where she wrote a number of short stories.

The Train Dogs

Out of the night and the north;
    Savage of breed and of bone,
Shaggy and swift comes the yelping band,
Freighters of fur from the voiceless land
    That sleeps in the Arctic zone.

Laden with skins from the north,
    Beaver and bear and raccoon,
Marten and mink from the polar belts,
Otter and ermine and sable pelts –
    The spoils of the hunter's moon.

Out of the night and the north,
    Sinewy, fearless and fleet,
Urging the pack through the pathless snow,
The Indian driver, calling low,
    Follows with moccasined feet.

Ships of the night and the north,
    Freighters on prairies and plains,
Carrying cargoes from field and flood
They scent the trail through their wild red
        blood,
    The wolfish blood in their veins.

E. PAULINE JOHNSON

BEN JONSON (1572-1637) was a British writer, the son of a bricklayer. He was a hot-headed quarrelsome man, but beloved of his friends. He was educated at Westminster, and after a short time spent as a bricklayer and later in military service he began work as a player and playwright in 1597. He is remembered for his lyrics and dramas. Many of his lyrics were set to music, among them Drink to Me Only With Thine Eyes, which appears in many current collections of familiar songs.

It is not growing like a tree

It is not growing like a tree
In bulk, doth make man better be;
Or standing long an oak, three hundred year,
To fall a log at last, dry, bald, and sear:
A lily of a day
Is fairer far in May,
Although it fall and die that night, –
It was the plant and flower of Light.
In small proportions we just beauties see,
And in short measures life may perfect be.

BEN JONSON

Still to be neat, still to be drest

Still to be neat, still to be drest,
As you were going to a feast;
Still to be powdered, still perfumed,
Lady, it is to be presumed,
Though art's hid causes are not found,
All is not sweet, all is not sound.

Give me a look, give me a face
That makes simplicity a grace;
Robes loosely flowing, hair as free:
Such sweet neglect more taketh me
Than all the adulteries of art;
They strike mine eyes, but not my heart.

BEN JONSON

JOHN KEATS (1795-1821): *Born in England, the son of a livery-stable keeper, Keats qualified in medicine before the age of 21. Giving up medicine for poetry, he produced a body of work in the five years remaining to him that established him as a major poet. After nursing a brother who died of tuberculosis, Keats contracted the disease and died aged twenty-six. He composed his own bitter epitaph: "Here lies one whose name was writ in water."*

The Eve of St. Agnes

1

St. Agnes' Eve – Ah, bitter chill it was!
The owl, for all his feathers, was a-cold;
The hare limped trembling through the frozen grass,
And silent was the flock in woolly fold:
Numb were the Beadsman's fingers, while he told
His rosary, and while his frosted breath,
Like pious incense from a censer old,
Seemed taking flight for heaven, without a death,
Past the sweet Virgin's picture, while his prayer he saith.

2

His prayer he saith, this patient, holy man;
Then takes his lamp, and riseth from his knees,
And back returneth, meager, barefoot, wan,
Along the chapel aisle by slow degrees:
The sculptured dead, on each side, seem to freeze,
Imprisoned in black, purgatorial rails:
Knights, ladies, praying in dumb orat'ries,
He passeth by; and his weak spirit fails
To think how they may ache in icy hoods and mails.

3

Northward he turneth through a little door,
And scarce three steps, ere Music's golden tongue
Flattered to tears this aged man and poor;
But no – already had his deathbell rung:
The joys of all his life were said and sung:
His was harsh penance on St. Agnes' Eve:
Another way he went, and soon among
Rough ashes sat he for his soul's reprieve,
And all night kept awake, for sinners' sake to grieve.

4

That ancient Beadsman heard the prelude soft;
And so it chanced, for many a door was wide,
From hurry to and fro. Soon, up aloft,
The silver, snarling trumpets 'gan to chide:
The level chambers, ready with their pride,
Were glowing to receive a thousand guests:
The carvèd angels, ever eager-eyed,
Stared, where upon their heads the cornice rests,
With hair blown back, and wings put crosswise on their
breasts.

5

At length burst in the argent revelry,
With plume, tiara, and all rich array,
Numerous as shadows haunting faerily
The brain, new stuffed, in youth, with triumphs gay
Of old romance. These let us wish away,
And turn, sole-thoughted, to one Lady there,
Whose heart had brooded, all that wintry day,
On love, and winged St. Agnes' saintly care,
As she had heard old dames full many times declare.

6

They told her how, upon St. Agnes' Eve,
Young virgins might have visions of delight,
And soft adorings from their loves receive
Upon the honeyed middle of the night,
If ceremonies due they did aright;
As, supperless to bed they must retire,
And couch supine their beauties, lily white;
Nor look behind, nor sideways, but require
Of Heaven with upward eyes for all that they desire.

7

Full of this whim was thoughtful Madeline:
The music, yearning like a God in pain,
She scarcely heard: her maiden eyes divine,
Fixed on the floor, saw many a sweeping train
Pass by – she heeded not at all: in vain
Came many a tiptoe, amorous cavalier,
And back retired; not cooled by high disdain;
But she saw not: her heart was otherwhere:
She sighed for Agnes' dreams, the sweetest of the year.

8

She danced along with vague, regardless eyes,
Anxious her lips, her breathing quick and short:
The hallowed hour was near at hand: she sighs
Amid the timbrels, and the thronged resort
Of whisperers in anger, or in sport;
'Mid looks of love, defiance, hate, and scorn,
Hoodwinked with faery fancy; all amort,
Save to St. Agnes and her lambs unshorn,
And all the bliss to be before tomorrow morn.

9

So, purposing each moment to retire,
She lingered still. Meantime, across the moors,
Had come young Porphyro, with heart on fire
For Madeline. Beside the portal doors,
Buttressed from moonlight, stands he, and implores
All saints to give him sight of Madeline,
But for one moment in the tedious hours,
That he might gaze and worship all unseen;
Perchance speak, kneel, touch, kiss – in sooth such things
                                        have been.

10

He ventures in: let no buzzed whisper tell:
All eyes be muffled, or a hundred swords
Will storm his heart, Love's fev'rous citadel:
For him, those chambers held barbarian hordes,
Hyena foemen, and hot-blooded lords,
Whose very dogs would execrations howl
Against his lineage: not one breast affords
Him any mercy, in that mansion foul,
Save one old beldame, weak in body and in soul.

11

Ah, happy chance! the aged creature came,
Shuffling along with ivory-headed wand,
To where he stood, hid from the torch's flame,
Behind a broad hall-pillar, far beyond
The sound of merriment and chorus bland:
He startled her; but soon she knew his face,
And grasped his fingers in her palsied hand,
Saying, "Mercy, Porphyro! hie thee from this place;
They are all here tonight, the whole bloodthirsty race!

12

"Get hence! get hence! there's dwarfish Hildebrand;
He had a fever late, and in the fit
He cursèd thee and thine, both house and land:
Then there's that old Lord Maurice, not a whit
More tame for his gray hairs – Alas me! flit!
Flit like a ghost away." – "Ah, Gossip dear,
We're safe enough; here in this armchair sit,
And tell me how" – "Good Saints! not here, not here;
Follow me, child, or else these stones will be thy bier."

13

He followed through a lowly archèd way,
Brushing the cobwebs with his lofty plume,
And as she muttered "Well-a – well-a-day!"
He found him in a little moonlight room,
Pale, latticed, chill, and silent as a tomb.
"Now tell me where is Madeline," said he,
"O tell me, Angela, by the holy loom
Which none but secret sisterhood may see,
When they St. Agnes' wool are weaving piously."

14

"St Agnes! Ah! it is St. Agnes' Eve –
Yet men will murder upon holy days:
Thou must hold water in a witch's sieve,
And be liege lord of all the Elves and Fays,
To venture so: it fills me with amaze
To see thee, Porphyro! – St. Agnes' Eve!
God's help! my lady fair the conjuror plays
This very night: good angels her deceive!
But let me laugh awhile, I've mickle time to grieve."

15

Feebly she laugheth in the languid moon,
While Porphyro upon her face doth look,
Like puzzled urchin on an aged crone
Who keepeth closed a wondrous riddle-book,
As spectacled she sits in chimney nook.
But soon his eyes grew brilliant, when she told
His lady's purpose; and he scarce could brook
Tears, at the thought of those enchantments cold,
And Madeline asleep in lap of legends old.

16

Sudden a thought came like a full-blown rose,
Flushing his brow, and in his painèd heart
Made purple riot: then doth he propose
A stratagem, that makes the beldame start:
"A cruel man and impious thou art:
Sweet lady, let her pray, and sleep, and dream
Alone with her good angels, far apart
From wicked men like thee. Go, go! – I deem
Thou canst not surely be the same that thou didst seem."

17

"I will not harm her, by all saints I swear,"
Quoth Porphyro: "O may I ne'er find grace
When my weak voice shall whisper its last prayer,
If one of her soft ringlets I displace,
Or look with ruffian passion in her face:
Good Angela, believe me by these tears;
Or I will, even in a moment's space,
Awake, with horrid shout, my foemen's ears,
And beard them, though they be more fanged than wolves
and bears."

18

"Ah! why wilt thou affright a feeble soul?
A poor, weak, palsy-stricken, churchyard thing,
Whose passing bell may ere the midnight toll;
Whose prayers for thee, each morn and evening,
Were never missed." – Thus plaining, doth she bring
A gentler speech from burning Porphyro;
So woeful and of such deep sorrowing,
That Angela gives promise she will do
Whatever he shall wish, betide her weal or woe.

19

Which was, to lead him, in close secrecy,
Even to Madeline's chamber, and there hide
Him in a closet, of such privacy
That he might see her beauty unespied,
And win perhaps that night a peerless bride,
While legioned faeries paced the coverlet,
And pale enchantment held her sleepy-eyed.
Never on such a night have lovers met,
Since Merlin paid his Demon all the monstrous debt.

20

"It shall be as thou wishest," said the Dame:
"All cates and dainties shall be storèd there
Quickly on this feast night: by the tambour frame
Her own lute thou wilt see: no time to spare,
For I am slow and feeble, and scarce dare
On such a catering trust my dizzy head.
Wait here, my child, with patience; kneel in prayer
The while: Ah! thou must needs the lady wed,
Or may I never leave my grave among the dead."

21

So saying, she hobbled off with busy fear.
The lover's endless minutes slowly passed:
The dame returned, and whispered in his ear
To follow her; with aged eyes aghast
From fright of dim espial. Safe at last,
Through many a dusky gallery, they gain
The maiden's chamber, silken, hushed, and chaste;
Where Porphyro took covert, pleased amain.
His poor guide hurried back with agues in her brain.

22

Her falt'ring hand upon the balustrade,
Old Angela was feeling for the stair,
When Madeline, St. Agnes' charmèd maid,
Rose, like a missioned spirit, unaware:
With silver taper's light, and pious care,
She turned, and down the aged gossip led
To a safe level matting. Now prepare,
Young Porphyro, for gazing on that bed;
She comes, she comes again, like ringdove frayed and fled.

23

Out went the taper as she hurried in;
Its little smoke, in pallid moonshine, died:
She closed the door, she panted, all akin
To spirits of the air, and visions wide:
No uttered syllable, or, woe betide!
But to her heart, her heart was voluble,
Paining with eloquence her balmy side;
As though a tongueless nightingale should swell
Her throat in vain, and die, heart-stifled, in her dell.

24

A casement high and triple-arched there was,
All garlanded with carven imag'ries
Of fruits, and flowers, and bunches of knot-grass,
And diamonded with panes of quaint device,
Innumerable of stains and splendid dyes,
As are the tiger-moth's deep-damasked wings;
And in the midst, 'mong thousand heraldries,
And twilight saints, and dim emblazonings,
A shielded scutcheon blushed with blood of queens and
kings.

25

Full on this casement shone the wintry moon,
And threw warm gules on Madeline's fair breast,
As down she knelt for heaven's grace and boon;
Rose-bloom fell on her hands, together pressed,
And on her silver cross soft amethyst,
And on her hair a glory, like a saint:
She seemed a splendid angel, newly dressed,
Save wings, for heaven – Porphyro grew faint:
She knelt, so pure a thing, so free from mortal taint.

26

Anon his heart revives: her vespers done,
Of all its wreathèd pearls her hair she frees;
Unclasps her warmèd jewels one by one;
Loosens her fragrant bodice; by degrees
Her rich attire creeps rustling to her knees:
Half-hidden, like a mermaid in sea-weed,
Pensive awhile she dreams awake, and sees,
In fancy, fair St. Agnes in her bed,
But dares not look behind, or all the charm is fled.

27

Soon, trembling in her soft and chilly nest,
In sort of wakeful swoon, perplexed she lay,
Until the poppied warmth of sleep oppressed
Her soothèd limbs, and soul fatigued away;
Flown, like a thought, until the morrow-day;
Blissfully havened both from joy and pain;
Clasped like a missal where swart Paynims pray;
Blinded alike from sunshine and from rain,
As though a rose should shut, and be a bud again.

28

Stol'n to this paradise, and so entranced,
Porphyro gazed upon her empty dress,
And listened to her breathing, if it chanced
To wake into a slumberous tenderness;
Which when he heard, that minute did he bless,
And breathed himself: then from the closet crept,
Noiseless as fear in a wide wilderness,
And over the hushed carpet, silent, stepped,
And 'tween the curtains peeped, where, lo!–how fast
                                        she slept.

29

Then by the bedside, where the faded moon
Made a dim, silver twilight, soft he set
A table, and, half anguished, threw thereon
A cloth of woven crimson, gold, and jet–
O for some drowsy Morphean amulet!
The boisterous, midnight, festive clarion,
The kettledrum, and far-heard clarinet,
Affray his ears, though but in dying tone–
The hall door shuts again, and all the noise is gone.

30

And still she slept an azure-lidded sleep,
In blanchèd linen, smooth, and lavendered,
While he from forth the closet brought a heap
Of candied apple, quince, and plum, and gourd;
With jellies soother than the creamy curd,
And lucent syrups, tinct with cinnamon;
Manna and dates, in argosy transferrred
From Fez; and spicèd dainties every one,
From silken Samarcand to cedared Lebanon.

31

These delicates he heaped with glowing hand
On golden dishes and in baskets bright
Of wreathèd silver: sumptuous they stand
In the retirèd quiet of the night,
Filling the chilly room with perfume light.–
"And now, my love, my seraph fair, awake!
Thou art my heaven, and I thine eremite:
Open thine eyes, for meek St. Agnes' sake,
Or I shall drowse beside thee, so my soul doth ache."

32

Thus whispering, his warm, unnervèd arm
Sank in her pillow. Shaded was her dream
By the dusk curtains: 'twas a midnight charm
Impossible to melt as icèd stream:
The lustrous salvers in the moonlight gleam;
Broad golden fringe upon the carpet lies:
It seemed he never, never could redeem
From such a steadfast spell his lady's eyes;
So mused awhile, entoiled in woofèd fantasies.

33

Awakening up, he took her hollow lute –
Tumultuous – and, in chords that tenderest be,
He played an ancient ditty, long since mute,
In Provence called *"La belle dame sans merci"*
Close to her ear touching the melody;
Wherewith disturbed, she uttered a soft moan:
He ceased – she panted quick – and suddenly
Her blue affrayèd eyes wide open shone:
Upon his knees he sank, pale as smooth-sculptured stone.

34

Her eyes were open, but she still beheld,
Now wide awake, the vision of her sleep:
There was a painful change, that nigh expelled
The blisses of her dream so pure and deep,
At which fair Madeline began to weep,
And moan forth witless words with many a sigh;
While still her gaze on Porphyro would keep,
Who knelt, with joinèd hands and piteous eye,
Fearing to move or speak, she looked so dreamingly.

35

"Ah, Porphyro!" said she, "but even now
Thy voice was at sweet tremble in mine ear,
Made tunable with every sweetest vow;
And those sad eyes were spiritual and clear:
How changed thou art! how pallid, chill, and drear!
Give me that voice again, my Porphyro,
Those looks immortal, those complainings dear!
Oh leave me not in this eternal woe,
For if thou diest, my Love, I know not where to go."

36

Beyond a mortal man impassioned far
At these voluptuous accents, he arose,
Ethereal, flushed, and like a throbbing star
Seen mid the sapphire heaven's deep repose;
Into her dream he melted, as the rose
Blendeth its odor with the violet –
Solution sweet: meantime the frost-wind blows
Like Love's alarum pattering the sharp sleet
Against the windowpanes; St. Agnes' moon hath set.

37

'Tis dark: quick pattereth the flaw-blown sleet:
"This is no dream, my bride, my Madeline!"
'Tis dark: the icèd gusts still rave and beat:
"No dream, alas! alas! and woe is mine!
Porphyro will leave me here to fade and pine. –
Cruel! what traitor could thee hither bring?
I curse not, for my heart is lost in thine,
Though thou foresakest a deceivèd thing –
A dove forlorn and lost with sick unprunèd wing."

38

"My Madeline! sweet dreamer! lovely bride!
Say, may I be for aye thy vassal blest?
Thy beauty's shield, heart-shaped and vermcil dyed?
Ah, silver shrine, here will I take my rest
After so many hours of toil and quest,
A famished pilgrim – saved by miracle.
Though I have found, I will not rob thy nest
Saving of thy sweet self; if thou think'st well
To trust, fair Madeline, to no rude infidel.

39

"Hark! 'tis an elfin-storm from faery land,
Of haggard seeming, but a boon indeed:
Arise – arise! the morning is at hand –
The bloated wassaillers will never heed –
Let us away, my love, with happy speed;
There are no ears to hear, or eyes to see –
Drowned all in Rhenish and the sleepy mead:
Awake! arise! my love, and fearless be,
For o'er the southern moors I have a home for thee."

40

She hurried at his words, beset with fears,
For there were sleeping dragons all around,
At glaring watch, perhaps, with ready spears –
Down the wide stairs a darkling way they found. –
In all the house was heard no human sound.
A chain-dropped lamp was flickering by each door;
The arras, rich with horseman, hawk, and hound,
Fluttered in the besieging wind's uproar;
And the long carpets rose along the gusty floor.

41

They glide, like phantoms, into the wide hall;
Like phantoms, to the iron porch, they glide;
Where lay the Porter, in uneasy sprawl,
With a huge empty flagon by his side:
The wakeful bloodhound rose, and shook his hide,
But his sagacious eye an inmate owns:
By one, and one, the bolts full easy slide:
The chains lie silent on the footworn stones;
The key turns, and the door upon its hinges groans.

42

And they are gone: aye, ages long ago
These lovers fled away into the storm.
That night the Baron dreamt of many a woe,
And all his warrior-guests, with shade and form
Of witch, and demon, and large coffin-worm,
Were long be-nightmared. Angela the old
Died palsy-twitched, with meager face deform;
The Beadsman, after thousand aves told,
For aye unsought for slept among his ashes cold.

JOHN KEATS

RUDYARD KIPLING (1865-1936) was born in India of English parents, but at age six he was sent to school in England, where he felt homesick and unhappy. He returned to India where he worked as a journalist and soon began to write poetry and short stories. He finally returned with his wife to England in 1916. An Empire-loyalist who greatly admired qualities of bravery, doggedness and self-sufficiency, he wrote delightfully about children and animals, his most famous tales being the Just So Stories *and the* Jungle Books.

L'Envoi

When Earth's last picture is painted and the tubes are twisted
    and dried,
When the oldest colours have faded, and the youngest critic
    has died,
We shall rest, and, faith, we shall need it – lie down for an
    aeon or two,
Till the Master of All Good Workmen shall put us to work
    anew!

And those that were good shall be happy: they shall sit in a
    golden chair;
They shall splash at a ten-league canvas with brushes of
    comets' hair.
They shall find real saints to draw from – Magdalene, Peter,
    and Paul;
They shall work for an age at a sitting and never be tired at
    all!

And only The Master shall praise us, and only The Master
    shall blame;
And no one shall work for money, and no one shall work for
    fame,
But each for the joy of the working, and each, in his separate
    star,
Shall draw the Thing as he sees It for the God of Things as
    They are!

RUDYARD KIPLING

RAYMOND KNISTER (1899-1932) *was born and raised on a farm in south-western Ontario. After attending the Universities of Toronto and Iowa State, he worked as an editor in the American mid-west, and later as a freelance writer in Toronto and Montreal. He was drowned at age thirty-three while on a summer holiday. The fact that Knister was one of the first Canadians to write skilful and meaningful poetry about daily farm life was not appreciated in his lifetime.*

The Colt

Through the gate
The boy leads him,
Turns him, expectant,
Around;
Slips off the halter:
He whirls, is gone,–
Boy brandishing
The halter at his going,
Clapping his hands–
Unnecessary–
In long lopes he speeds,
Rising and dipping,
Down the rolling lane.
Such beauty, see,
Such grace,
Moving (diversely!)
Never was.
Nor such gait-perfection
And exactness
Is in any man.
His mane and his tail
Lie back on the breeze,
And the breeze at his every lope
Surges past
His laid-back ears.
See the long swift
Flash and swing,
Low,
Of his limbs . . .
Gone now,

But back streaks his whinny
Wild, enimaging himself;
He will round the gate corner
At the end of the long pasture
With entrancing ease
And speed,
Re-accelerate,
Bound onward to his comrades,
And stop.
Or else, breaking
Into a great high free stride,
Trot up to, around them,
Tail up, nose inheld;
Greet his kinsfolk.
The farmer looks over his fence
To see him pass;
And his world,
And its days, make him say:
"Idle colts!
Somehow nohow of any use!"

RAYMOND KNISTER

JOY KOGAWA (1935-   ) was born in Vancouver of Japanese ancestry. Her family was among those uprooted and settled in Lethbridge during the Second World War. She has published several books of prose and poetry, among them the novel Obasan, *which is about the expulsion of the Japanese during the war.*

When I Was a Little Girl

When I was a little girl
We used to walk together
Tim, my brother who wore glasses,
And I, holding hands
Tightly as we crossed the bridge
And he'd murmur, 'You pray now'
— being a clergyman's son —
Until the big white boys
Had kicked on past.
Later we'd climb the bluffs
Overhanging the ghost town
And pick the small white lilies
And fling them like bombers
Over Slocan.

JOY KOGAWA

Unfolding Bud

One is amazed
By a water-lily bud
Unfolding
With each passing day,
Taking on a richer color
And new dimensions.

One is not amazed,
At a first glance,
By a poem,
Which is as tight-closed
As a tiny bud.

Yet one is surprised
To see the poem
Gradually unfolding,
Revealing its rich inner self,
As one reads it
Again
And over again.

NAOSHI KORIYAMA

D.H. LAWRENCE (1885-1930) was born in an English coal-mining village, where he experienced a miserable childhood at the hands of his alcoholic father. Frail and studious, he worked as a teacher before devoting himself to writing.
In 1912 he fell in love with Frieda Weekley, a married German woman who agreed to live with him. They were finally married in 1914, travelled widely, and had a stormy but enduring relationship until his death at age forty-four of tuberculosis. Lawrence's entire work was devoted to the pursuit of a fuller, freer, more intense life than is permitted by our industrial civilization and social system.

Mountain Lion

Climbing through the January snow, into the Lobo
    canyon
Dark grow the spruce-trees, blue is the balsam, water
    sounds still unfrozen, and the trail is still evident.

Men!
Two men!
Men! The only animal in the world to fear!

They hesitate.
We hesitate.
They have a gun.
We have no gun.

Then we all advance, to meet.
Two Mexicans, strangers, emerging out of the dark
    and snow and inwardness of the Lobo valley.
What are you doing here on this vanishing trail?

What is he carrying?
Something yellow.
A deer?

¿ Que tiene, amigo?
León –

He smiles, foolishly, as if he were caught doing wrong.
And we smile, foolishly, as if we didn't know.
He is quite gentle and dark-faced.

It is a mountain lion,
A long, long slim cat, yellow like a lioness.
Dead.
He trapped her this morning, he says, smiling foolishly.

Lift up her face,
Her round, bright face, bright as frost.
Her round, fine-fashioned head, with two dead ears;
And stripes in the brilliant frost of her face, sharp, fine
    dark rays,
Dark, keen, fine eyes in the brilliant frost of her face.
Beautiful dead eyes.

   Hermoso es!

They go out towards the open;
We go on into the gloom of Lobo.
And above the trees I found her lair,
A hole in the blood-orange brilliant rocks that stick up,
    a little cave.
And bones, and twigs, and a perilous ascent.

So, she will never leap up that way again, with the yellow
    flash of a mountain lion's long shoot!
And her bright striped frost-face will never watch any more,
    out of the shadow of the cave in the blood-orange rock,
Above the trees of the Lobo dark valley-mouth!
Instead, I look out.
And out to the dim of the desert, like a dream, never
    real;

To the snow of the Sangre de Cristo mountains, the ice
    of the mountains of Picoris,
And near across at the opposite steep of snow, green trees
    motionless standing in snow, like a Christmas toy.

And I think in this empty world there was room for me
    and a mountain lion.
And I think in the world beyond, how easily we might
    spare a million or two of humans
And never miss them.
Yet what a gap in the world, the missing white frost-face
    of that slim yellow mountain lion!

D.H. LAWRENCE

Things Made by Iron

Things made by iron and handled by steel
are born dead, they are shrouds, they soak life out of us.
Till after a long time, when they are old
    and have steeped in our life
they begin to be soothed and soothing:
    then we throw them away.

D.H. LAWRENCE

Things Men Have Made

Things men have made with wakened hands, and put
    soft life into
are awake through years with transferred touch, and go
    on glowing
for long years.
And for this reason, some old things are lovely
warm still with the life of forgotten men who made
    them.

D.H. LAWRENCE

HENRY LEIGH (1837-1883) was born in London, the son of an artist. In addition to writing several volumes of light verse ("fluent but slight lyrics") he translated and adapted French comic opera for the British stage.

The Twins

In form and feature, face and limb,
    I grew so like my brother,
That folks got taking me for him,
    And each for one another.
It puzzled all our kith and kin,
    It reached an awful pitch;
For one of us was born a twin,
    Yet not a soul knew which.

One day (to make the matter worse),
    Before our names were fixed,
As we were being washed by nurse
    We got completely mixed;
And thus, you see, by Fate's decree,
    (Or rather nurse's whim),
My brother John got christened *me*,
    And I got christened *him*.

The fatal likeness even dogged
    My footsteps when at school,
And I was always getting flogged,
    For John turned out a fool.
I put this question hopelessly
    To everyone I knew–
What *would* you do, if you were me,
    To prove that you were *you*?

Our close resemblance turned the tide
    Of my domestic life;
For somehow my intended bride
    Became my brother's wife.
In short, year after year the same
    Absurd mistakes went on;
And when I died – the neighbours came
    And buried brother John!

HENRY LEIGH

DENISE LEVERTOV (1923-   ): Born in England, Levertov published her first book of poems at age twenty-three. She later married an American novelist and settled in the U.S.A. Her second book of poetry was in the Pocket Poets series launched by Lawrence Ferlinghetti.

Flute Music

(from *Six Variations*)

two flutes!   How close
to each other they move
in mazing figures,
never touching, never
breaking the measure,
as gnats dance in
summer haze all afternoon, over
shallow water sprinkled
with mottled blades of willow –
two flutes!

DENISE LEVERTOV

VACHEL LINDSAY (1879-1931) was born in Illinois of a pioneer family who practised a strongly social Christianity. Lindsay tried the priesthood and later art before deciding on a career in literary evangelism. He had much success, but his effective career was short. Details of his last years are sketchy. He took his own life in 1931.

The Flower-Fed Buffaloes

The flower-fed buffaloes of the spring
In the days of long ago,
Ranged where the locomotives sing
And the prairie flowers lie low: –
The tossing, blooming, perfumed grass
Is swept away by the wheat,
Wheels and wheels and wheels spin by
In the spring that still is sweet.
But the flower-fed buffaloes of the spring
Left us, long ago.
They gore no more, they bellow no more,
They trundle around the hills no more: –
With the Blackfeet, lying low,
With the Pawnees, lying low,
Lying low.

VACHEL LINDSAY

The Leaden-Eyed

Let not young souls be smothered out before
They do quaint deeds and fully flaunt their pride.
It is the world's one crime its babes grow dull,
Its poor are ox-like, limp, and leaden-eyed.
Not that they starve, but starve so dreamlessly;
Not that they sow, but that they seldom reap;
Not that they serve, but have no gods to serve;
Not that they die, but that they die like sheep.

VACHEL LINDSAY

HENRY WADSWORTH LONGFELLOW (1807-1882) was an American poet and translator, a professor of modern foreign languages. A simple and kindly man, he is one of the most popular poets America ever produced. His verse is conventional, rather sentimental, and easily memorized.

Nature

As a fond mother, when the day is o'er,
Leads by the hand her little child to bed,
Half willing, half reluctant to be led,
And leave his broken playthings on the floor,
Still gazing at them through the open door,
Nor wholly reassured and comforted
By promises of others in their stead.
Which, though more splendid, may not please
      him more;
So Nature deals with us, and takes away
Our playthings one by one, and by the hand
Leads us to rest so gently, that we go
Scarce knowing if we wish to go or stay.

HENRY WADSWORTH LONGFELLOW

MALCOLM LOWRY (1909-1957) was born in England. At seven-teen he sailed to the Far East as a deckhand on a freighter. Returning to England he graduated from Cambridge in English and Classics, travelled in Spain, and then to Hollywood where he wrote film scripts for a time. After spending a short time in Mexico he went to British Columbia in 1939, where he lived in a beach shack until 1954. He died in England.

Kingfishers in
British Columbia

A mad kingfisher
rocketing about in the
red fog at sunrise

now sits
on the alder
post that tethers the floats
angrily awaiting his mate.
Here she

comes, like a left wing
three-quarter cutting through toward
the goal in sun-lamped
fog at Rosslyn Park at half
past three in halcyon days.

MALCOLM LOWRY

Marshall

It occurred to Marshall
that if he were a vegetable, he'd
be a bean. Not
one of your thin, stringy
green beans, or your

dry, marbly
Burlotti beans. No, he'd be
a broad bean,
a rich, nutritious,
meaningful bean,

alert for advantages,
inquisitive with potatoes,
mixing with every kind
and condition of vegetable,
and a good friend

to meat and lager. Yes, he'd
leap from his huge
rough pod with a loud
popping sound
into the pot: always

in hot water
and out of it with a soft
heart inside
his horny carapace. He'd
carry the whole

world's hunger on
his broad shoulders, green
with best butter
or brown with gravy. And if
some starving Indian saw his

flesh bleeding
when the gas was turned on
or the knife went in
he'd accept the homage and prayers,
and become a god, and die like a man,

which, as things were, wasn't so easy.

GEORGE MACBETH

The Tom-Cat

At midnight in the alley
  A Tom-cat comes to wail,
And he chants the hate of a million years
  As he swings his snaky tail.

Malevolent, bony, brindled,
  Tiger and devil and bard,
His eyes are coals from the middle of Hell
  And his heart is black and hard.

He twists and crouches and capers
  And bares his curved sharp claws,
And he sings to the stars of the jungle nights
  Ere cities were, or laws.

Beast from a world primeval,
  He and his leaping clan,
When the blotched red moon leers over the roofs,
  Give voice to their scorn of man.

He will lie on a rug to-morrow
  And lick his silky fur.
And veil the brute in his yellow eyes
  And play he's tame, and purr.

But at midnight in the alley
  He will crouch again and wail,
And beat the time for his demon's song
  With the swing of his demon's tail.

DON MARQUIS

ANNE MARRIOTT (1913-   ) was born in Victoria, British Columbia. She now lives in Vancouver, writing and doing poetry workshops with students. She has written numerous school broadcasts and other scripts for the CBC. She and her husband adopted three children.

From "The Wind Our Enemy"

Wind
flattening its gaunt furious self against
the naked siding, knifing in the wounds
of time, pausing to tear aside the last
old scab of paint.

Wind
surging down the cocoa-coloured seams
of summer-fallow, darting in about
white hoofs and brown, snatching the sweaty cap
shielding red eyes.

Wind
filling the dry mouth with bitter dust
whipping the shoulders worry-bowed too soon,
soiling the water pail, and in grim prophecy
greying the hair.

. . . .

Wind
in a lonely laughterless shrill game
with broken wash-boiler, bucket without
a handle, Russian thistle, throwing up
sections of soil.

God, will it never rain again? What about
those clouds out west? No, that's just dust, as thick
and stifling now as winter underwear.
No rain, no crop, no feed, no faith, only
wind.

ANNE MARRIOTT

JOHN MASEFIELD (1878-1967) was born in England. Before he was twenty he had travelled widely as a merchant seaman, worked in a bakery, a stable, and a saloon in New York, and for two years in a carpet factory in Yonkers. Here he began to read widely and to write poems and essays of his own. He returned to London to set out on a literary career, where he built up a firm reputation as a novelist, poet, playwright, and nautical historian.

Cargoes

Quinquireme of Nineveh from distant Ophir
Rowing home to haven in sunny Palestine,
    With a cargo of ivory,
    And apes and peacocks,
Sandalwood, cedarwood, and sweet white wine.

Stately Spanish galleon coming from the Isthmus,
Dipping through the Tropics by the palm-green
    shores,
    With a cargo of diamonds,
    Emeralds, amethysts,
Topazes, and cinnamon, and gold moidores.

Dirty British coaster with a salt-caked smoke stack
Butting through the Channel in the mad March
    days,
    With a cargo of Tyne coal,
    Road rail, pig lead,
Firewood, ironware, and cheap tin trays.

JOHN MASEFIELD

Sea-Fever

I must go down to the seas again, to the lonely sea
 and the sky,
And all I ask is a tall ship and a star to steer her by,
And the wheel's kick and the wind's song and the
 white sail's shaking,
And a grey mist on the sea's face and a grey dawn
 breaking.

I must go down to the seas again, for the call of the
 running tide
Is a wild call and a clear call that may not be
 denied;
And all I ask is a windy day with the white clouds
 flying,
And the flung spray and the blown spume, and the
 sea-gulls crying.

I must go down to the seas again, to the vagrant
 gypsy life,
To the gull's way and the whale's way where the
 wind's like a whetted knife;
And all I ask is a merry yarn from a laughing
 fellow-rover,
And a quiet sleep and a sweet dream when the long
 trick's over.

JOHN MASEFIELD

EDGAR LEE MASTERS (1868-1950) was a Kansas-born lawyer. He had published some blank verse when, at the age of forty-seven, he was suddenly catapulted to fame with the publication of Spoon River Anthology, *a collection of epitaphs revealing the secret lives of the people buried in a fictional mid-western cemetery. He was also a biographer and a novelist.*

Silence

I have known the silence of the stars and of the sea,
And the silence of the city when it pauses,
And the silence of a man and a maid,
And the silence of the sick
When their eyes roam about the room.
And I ask: For the depths
Of what use is language?
A beast of the field moans a few times
When death takes its young.
And we are voiceless in the presence of realities –
We cannot speak.

A curious boy asks an old soldier
Sitting in front of the grocery store,
"How did you lose your leg?"
And the old soldier is struck with silence,
Or his mind flies away
Because he cannot concentrate it on Gettysburg.
It comes back jocosely
And he says, "A bear bit it off."
And the boy wonders, while the old soldier
Dumbly, feebly lives over
The flashes of guns, the thunder of cannon,
The shrieks of the slain,
And himself lying on the ground,
And the hospital surgeons, the knives,
And the long days in bed.
But if he could describe it all
He would be an artist.

But if he were an artist there would be deeper wounds
Which he could not describe.

There is the silence of a great hatred,
And the silence of a great love,
And the silence of an embittered friendship.
There is the silence of a spiritual crisis,
Through which your soul, exquisitely tortured,
Comes with visions not to be uttered
Into a realm of higher life.
There is the silence of defeat.
There is the silence of those unjustly punished;
And the silence of the dying whose hand
Suddenly grips yours.
There is the silence between father and son,
When the father cannot explain his life,
Even though he be misunderstood for it.

There is the silence that comes between husband and wife.
There is the silence of those who have failed;
And the vast silence that covers
Broken nations and vanquished leaders.
There is the silence of Lincoln,
Thinking of the poverty of his youth.
And the silence of Napoleon
After Waterloo.
And the silence of Jeanne d'Arc
Saying amid the flames, "Blessed Jesus"–
Revealing in two words all sorrows, all hope.
And there is the silence of age,
Too full of wisdom for the tongue to utter it
In words intelligible to those who have not lived
The great range of life.

And there is the silence of the dead.
If we who are in life cannot speak
Of profound experiences,
Why do you marvel that the dead
Do not tell you of death?
Their silence shall be interpreted
As we approach them.

EDGAR LEE MASTERS

ROGER McGOUGH (1937-) was born in Liverpool, England. His "Pop Poetry" was at first much criticized, but his high spirits and great capacity for punning has since found many admirers. "The Scaffold," the humour, poetry and music group with which he worked, once topped the English hit parade.

40——Love

middle	aged
couple	playing
ten	nis
when	the
game	ends
and	they
go	home
the	net
will	still
be	be
tween	them

ROGER McGOUGH

JOSEPH McLEOD (1929-   ) was born in Hamilton, Ontario. He works as a teacher, farmer and artistic director of the Peterborough summer theatre. He writes drama as well as poetry.

I
like to
live
by a lake

Water
is good

Always looking at
land
is
to live
without
stretch

JOSEPH McLEOD

Then the Child Replied

The soldier said,
I have worked today.
I have killed three men
and burned many fields.

The men here die easily.

I am hungry.
Now sprawled at
the side of the road
in this land,
I will eat.

I have meat, chocolate, coffee.

Oh yes, coffee from Brazil!
We get the best.
Why not? We do difficult tasks.

The children of this country are the
only things that seem real to me.
Take this bunch chirping and begging about me
now: surely, they look different
from my own children, still they act like
my children, – hungry birds.

You take that one over there, the one
holding back, the one with the weasel eyes;
he wants some of my food, and I would give
him some, but as I said, I worked today and
am hungry.

I do not know why
I kill these particular people
in this strange country:
I just do my job.

The children are coming closer now . . .
He watches . . . Oh, how he watches . . .
As always, I think of my own children and
my heart melts with compassion,
and although I am hungry and
love chocolate best,
I offer some to this weasel child.

Then the child replied,
'No thank you, soldier,
I do not like chocolate anymore.'

JOSEPH McLEOD

EVE MERRIAM (1916-　　) was born in Philadelphia and started her writing career as a copywriter and radio writer. She has published plays and children's fiction in addition to her poetry. She says, "I am fortunate in that my work is my main pleasure, and, while I find all forms of writing absorbing, I like poetry as the most immediate and richest form of communication."

How To Eat a Poem

Don't be polite.
Bite in.
Pick it up with your fingers and lick the juice
    that may run down your chin.
It is ready and ripe now, whenever you are.

You do not need a knife or fork or spoon
or plate or napkin or tablecloth.

For there is no core
or stem
or rind
or pit
or seed
or skin
to throw away.

EVE MERRIAM

CHARLOTTE MEW (1870-1928) was born in England and spent
most of her life in poverty. Mental instability in the family,
and the deaths of her parents and siblings, the last being her
dearest sister whom she had nursed for some time, led to
Mew's eventual suicide at age fifty-seven. It has been written
of her: "Her wind-blown grey hair, her startled grey eyes, her
thin white face, belonged to a reluctant visitor from another
world frightened at what she had undergone in this one."
Her friendship with Thomas Hardy was "the only joyous
thing that ever happened to her."

The Changeling

Toll no bell for me, dear Father, dear Mother,
　　Waste no sighs;
There are my sisters, there is my little brother
　　Who plays in the place called Paradise,
Your children all, your children for ever;
　　But I, so wild,
Your disgrace, with the queer brown face, was
　　never,
　　Never, I know, but half your child!
In the garden at play, all day, last summer,
　　Far and away I heard
The sweet "tweet-tweet" of a strange new-comer,
　　The dearest, clearest call of a bird.

It lived down there in the deep green hollow,
　　My own old home, and the fairies say
The word of a bird is a thing to follow,
　　So I was away a night and a day.

One evening, too, by the nursery fire,
　　We snuggled close and sat round so still,
When suddenly as the wind blew higher,
　　Something scratched on the window-sill.
A pinched brown face peered in – I shivered;
　　No one listened or seemed to see;
The arms of it waved and the wings of it quivered.
　　Whoo – I knew it had come for me!

Some are as bad as bad can be!
All night long they danced in the rain,
Round and round in a dripping chain,
Threw their caps at the window-pane,
  Tried to make me scream and shout
  And fling the bedclothes all about:
I meant to stay in bed that night,
And if only you had left a light
  They would never have got me out!

Sometimes I wouldn't speak, you see,
  Or answer when you spoke to me,
Because in the long, still dusks of Spring
You can hear the whole world whispering;
  The shy green grasses making love,
  The feathers grow on the dear grey dove,
  The tiny heart of the redstart beat,
  The patter of the squirrel's feet,
The pebbles pushing in the silver streams,
The rushes talking in their dreams,
  The swish-swish of the bat's black wings,
  The wild-wood bluebell's sweet ting-tings,
    Humming and hammering at your ear,
    Everything there is to hear
In the heart of hidden things.
  But not in the midst of the nursery riot,
  That's why I wanted to be quiet,
    Couldn't do my sums, or sing,
    Or settle down to anything.
  And when, for that, I was sent upstairs
  I *did* kneel down to say my prayers;
But the King who sits on your high church steeple
Has nothing to do with us fairy people!
'Times I pleased you, dear Father, dear Mother.
  Learned all my lessons and liked to play,
And dearly I loved the little pale brother
  Whom some other bird must have called away.
Why did they bring me here to make me
  Not quite bad and not quite good,

Why, unless They're wicked, do They want, in
    spite, to take me
      Back to Their wet, wild wood?
Now, every night I shall see the windows shining,
  The gold lamp's glow, and the fire's red gleam,
When the best of us are twining twigs and the rest
    of us are whining
      In the hollow by the stream.
Black and chill are Their nights on the wold;
  And They live so long and They feel no pain:
I shall grow up, but never grow old,
I shall always, always be very cold,
      I shall never come back again!

CHARLOTTE MEW

ALICE MEYNELL (1847-1922) was born in London of a wealthy family. In 1877 she married journalist Wilfred Meynell, and thereafter lived a life of hard work and relative poverty. The marriage was, however, a particularly happy one. In spite of the cares of raising eight children, and the problem of repeated migraine headaches, Meynell published a good deal of work (for which she was once seriously considered as Poet Laureate). She was an ardent feminist "in lawful and dignified ways."

Maternity

One wept whose only child was dead,
    Newborn, ten years ago.
'Weep not; he is in bliss,' they said.
    She answered, 'Even so.

'Ten years ago was born in pain
    A child, not now forlorn.
But oh, ten years ago, in vain,
    A mother, a mother was born.'

ALICE MEYNELL

City Trees

The trees along this city street,
    Save for the traffic and the trains,
Would make a sound as thin and sweet
    As trees in country lanes.

And people standing in their shade
    Out of a shower, undoubtedly
Would hear such music as is made
    Upon a country tree.

Oh, little leaves that are so dumb
    Against the shrieking city air,
I watch you when the wind has come,–
    I know what sound is there.

EDNA ST. VINCENT MILLAY

From "A Few Figs from Thistles"

First Fig

My candle burns at both ends;
   It will not last the night;
But ah, my foes, and oh, my friends ~
   It gives a lovely light!

Second Fig

Safe upon the solid rock the ugly houses stand:
Come and see my shining palace built upon the sand!

EDNA ST. VINCENT MILLAY

Lament

Listen, children:
Your father is dead.
From his old coats
I'll make you little jackets;
I'll make you little trousers
From his old pants.
There'll be in his pockets
Things he used to put there,
Keys and pennies
Covered with tobacco;
Dan shall have the pennies
To save in his bank;
Anne shall have the keys
To make a pretty noise with.
Life must go on,
And the dead be forgotten;
Life must go on,
Tho good men die;
Anne, eat your breakfast;
Dan, take your medicine;
Life must go on;
I forget just why.

EDNA ST. VINCENT MILLAY

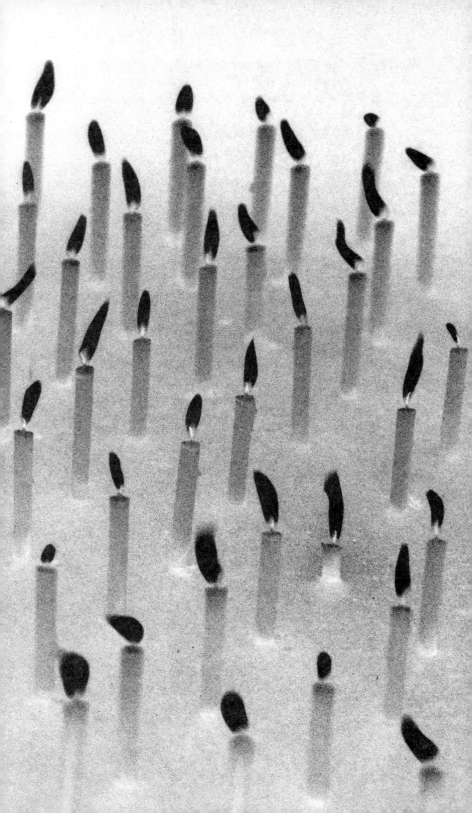

The Horses

Barely a twelvemonth after
The seven days war that put the world to sleep,
Late in the evening the strange horses came.
By then we had made our covenant with silence,
But in the first few days it was so still
We listened to our breathing and were afraid.
On the second day
The radios failed; we turned the knobs; no answer.
On the third day a warship passed us, heading north,
Dead bodies piled on the deck. On the sixth day
A plane plunged over us into the sea. Thereafter
Nothing. The radios dumb;
And still they stand in corners of our kitchens,
And stand, perhaps, turned on, in a million rooms
All over the world. But now, if they should speak,
If on a sudden they should speak again,
If on the stroke of noon a voice should speak,
We would not listen, we would not let it bring
That old bad world that swallowed its children quick
At one great gulp. We would not have it again.
Sometimes we think of the nations lying asleep,
Curled blindly in impenetrable sorrow,
And then the thought confounds us with its strangeness.

The tractors lie about our fields; at evening
They look like dank sea-monsters couched and waiting.
We leave them where they are and let them rust:
'They'll moulder away and be like other loam'.
We make our oxen drag our rusty ploughs,

Long laid aside. We have gone back
Far past our fathers' land.

                                And then, that evening
Late in the summer the strange horses came.
We heard a distant tapping on the road,
A deepening drumming; it stopped, went on again
And at the corner changed to hollow thunder.
We saw the heads
Like a wild wave charging and were afraid.
We had sold our horses in our fathers' time
To buy new tractors. Now they were strange to us
As fabulous steeds set on an ancient shield
Or illustrations in a book of knights.
We did not dare go near them. Yet they waited,
Stubborn and shy, as if they had been sent
By an old command to find our whereabouts
And that long-lost archaic companionship
In the first moment we had never a thought
That they were creatures to be owned and used.
Among them were some half-a-dozen colts
Dropped in some wilderness of the broken world,
Yet new as if they had come from their own Eden.
Since then they have pulled our ploughs and borne our loads,
But that free servitude still can pierce our hearts.
Our life is changed; their coming our beginning.

EDWIN MUIR

I Have Always Known

I have always known
That at last I would
Take this road, but yesterday
I did not know that it would be today.

NARIHIRA
(TRANSLATED BY KENNETH REXROTH)

JOHN NEWLOVE (1938-   ) was born in Regina and spent his early years in eastern Saskatchewan. Some of his work displays an almost racial memory of the Prairies as they were before the colonists arrived. He is often the outsider in his work, the loser in a threatening world where the only thing to do is to keep moving. Newlove has held a variety of jobs, including writer-in-residence at three universities.

The Hitchhiker

On that black highway,
where are you going? –

It is in Alberta
among the trees

where the road sweeps
left and right

in great concrete arcs
at the famous resort –

there you stood on
the road in the wind

the cold wind going
through you and you

going through the country
to no end, only

to turn again at one sea
and begin it again,

feeling safe with strangers
in a moving car.

JOHN NEWLOVE

HERBERT NEWMAN (1925-   ) is an American composer, author and record company executive. In collaboration with Stan Lebowsky he has written, published and recorded a number of songs, of which The Wayward Wind is probably the best known.

The Wayward Wind

Oh the wayward wind is a restless wind,
A restless wind that yearns to wander;
And he was born the next of kin,
The next of kin to the wayward wind.

In a lonely shack by the railroad track
He spent his younger days,
And I guess the sound of the outward bound
Made him a slave to the wandering ways.

Oh I met him there in a border town;
He vowed we'd never part.
Though he tried his best to settle down
Now I'm alone with a broken heart.

And the wayward wind is a restless wind,
A restless wind that yearns to wander;
And he was born the next of kin,
The next of kin to the wayward wind.

HERBERT NEWMAN,
WITH STAN LEBOWSKY

A.D. 2267

Once on the gritty moon (burnt earth hung far
In the black, rhinestone sky – lopsided star),
Two gadgets, with great fishbowls for a head,
Feet clubbed, hips loaded, shoulders bent. She said,
"Fantasies haunt me. A green garden. Two
Lovers aglow in flesh. The pools so blue!"
He whirrs with masculine pity, "Can't forget
Old superstitions? The earth-legend yet?"

JOHN FREDERICK NIMS (1913-   )

ALDEN NOWLAN (1933-   ) was born in Nova Scotia. He left school at age twelve and worked as a farm labourer and manager of a hillbilly orchestra before turning to journalism. Much of his writing has been on the Puritan distrust of joy he finds in the small-town people of the Maritimes. He says, "I am a product of a culture that fears any display of emotion and attempts to repress any true communication . . . I think the most important division in the world is between the people who are real and the people who are fakes."

A Note on the Public Transportation System

It's not hard to begin
a conversation with the person
who happens to be seated
nearest you, especially when she's been
reading with apparent interest
a book that's one of your
favourites and can't find
her matches.
          The difficulty is
once you've spoken you can never
go back to being comfortable
with silence,
          even if you learn
you've nothing to say
and would rather not listen.
          You can stop talking
but you can't forget
the broken wires
dangling there between you.
          You'll smile almost guiltily
when your glances
accidentally bump.
          It may get so bad
that one of you will have to
pretend to fall asleep.

ALDEN NOWLAN

The Bull Moose

Down from the purple mist of trees on the mountain,
lurching through forests of white spruce and cedar,
stumbling through tamarack swamps,
came the bull moose
to be stopped at last by a pole-fenced pasture.

Too tired to turn or, perhaps, aware
there was no place left to go, he stood with the cattle.
They, scenting the musk of death, seeing his great head
like the ritual mask of a blood god, moved to the other end
of the field, and waited.

The neighbours heard of it, and by afternoon
cars lined the road. The children teased him
with alder switches and he gazed at them
like an old, tolerant collie. The woman asked
if he could have escaped from a Fair.

The oldest man in the parish remembered seeing
a gelded moose yoked with an ox for plowing.
The young men snickered and tried to pour beer
down his throat, while their girl friends took their pictures.

And the bull moose let them stroke his tick-ravaged flanks,
let them pry open his jaws with bottles, let a giggling girl
plant a little purple cap
of thistles on his head.

When the wardens came, everyone agreed it was a shame
to shoot anything so shaggy and cuddlesome.
He looked like the kind of pet
women put to bed with their sons.

So they held their fire. But just as the sun dropped in the river
the bull moose gathered his strength
like a scaffolded king, straightened and lifted his horns
so that even the wardens backed away as they raised their rifles.
When he roared, people ran to their cars. All the young men
leaned on their automobile horns as he toppled.

ALDEN NOWLAN

Warren Pryor

When every pencil meant a sacrifice
his parents boarded him at school in town,
slaving to free him from the stony fields,
the meagre acreage that bore them down.

They blushed with pride when, at his graduation,
they watched him picking up the slender scroll,
his passport from the years of brutal toil
and lonely patience in a barren hole.

When he went in the Bank their cups ran over.
They marvelled how he wore a milk-white shirt
work days and jeans on Sundays. He was saved
from their thistle-strewn farm and its red dirt.

And he said nothing. Hard and serious
like a young bear inside his teller's cage,
his axe-hewn hands upon the paper bills
aching with empty strength and throttled rage.

ALDEN NOWLAN

ALFRED NOYES (1880-1958): **Born in England, educated at Oxford, Noyes first made his mark as a poet in London. His epic poem** Drake **appeared in** Blackwoods Magazine *like a serial novel, each episode being eagerly awaited by the public. He is known chiefly as a writer of national epics and stirring ballads. He was very critical of "false intellectuals," as he called the main writers of his time.*

The Highwayman

PART ONE

The wind was a torrent of darkness among the gusty trees,
The moon was a ghostly galleon tossed upon cloudy seas,
The road was a ribbon of moonlight over the purple moor.
And the highwayman came riding –
     Riding – riding –
The highwayman came riding, up to the old inn-door.

He'd a French cocked-hat on his forehead, a bunch of lace
    at his chin,
A coat of the claret velvet, and breeches of brown doe-skin;
They fitted with never a wrinkle: his boots were up to
    the thigh!
And he rode with a jewelled twinkle,
     His pistol butts a-twinkle,
His rapier hilt a-twinkle, under the jewelled sky.

Over the cobbles he clattered and clashed in the dark
    inn-yard,
And he tapped with his whip on the shutters, but all was
    locked and barred;
He whistled a tune to the window, and who should be
    waiting there
But the landlord's black-eyed daughter,
     Bess, the landlord's daughter,
Plaiting a dark red love-knot into her long black hair.

And dark in the dark old inn-yard a stable-wicket creaked
Where Tim the ostler listened; his face was white and
　　　peaked;
His eyes were hollows of madness, his hair like mouldy hay,
But he loved the landlord's daughter,
　　　　　The landlord's red-lipped daughter.
Dumb as a dog he listened, and he heard the robber say –

"One kiss, my bonny sweetheart, I'm after a prize to-night,
But I shall be back with the yellow gold before the morn-
　　　ing light;
Yet, if they press me sharply, and harry me through the
　　　day,
Then look for me by moonlight,
　　　　　Watch for me by moonlight,
I'll come to thee by moonlight, though hell should bar
　　　the way."

He rose upright in the stirrups; he scarce could reach her
　　　hand,
But she loosened her hair i' the casement!　His face burnt
　　　like a brand
As the black cascade of perfume came tumbling over his
　　　breast;
And he kissed its waves in the moonlight,
　　　　　(Oh, sweet black waves in the moonlight!)
Then he tugged at his rein in the moonlight, and galloped
　　　away to the West.

PART TWO

He did not come in the dawning; he did not come at noon;
And out o' the tawny sunset, before the rise o' the moon,
When the road was a gipsy's ribbon, looping the purple
　　　moor,
A red-coat troop came marching –
　　　　　Marching – marching –
King George's men came marching, up to the old inn-door.

They said no word to the landlord, they drank his ale
　　　instead,

But they gagged his daughter and bound her to the foot
    of her narrow bed;
Two of them knelt at her casement, with muskets at their
    side!
There was death at every window;
        And hell at one dark window;
For Bess could see, through her casement, the road that
    he would ride.

They had tied her up to attention, with many a sniggering
    jest;
They had bound a musket beside her, with the barrel
    beneath her breast!
"Now keep good watch!" and they kissed her. She
    heard the dead man say –
Look for me by moonlight;
    Watch for me by moonlight;
I'll come to thee by moonlight, though hell should bar
    the way!

She twisted her hands behind her; but all the knots held
    good!
She writhed her hands till her fingers were wet with sweat
    or blood!
They stretched and strained in the darkness, and the hours
    crawled by like years,
Till, now, on the stroke of midnight,
        Cold, on the stroke of midnight,
The tip of one finger touched it! The trigger at least
    was hers!

The tip of one finger touched it; she strove no more for
    the rest!
Up, she stood up to attention, with the barrel beneath her
    breast,
She would not risk their hearing; she would not strive
    again;
For the road lay bare in the moonlight;
        Blank and bare in the moonlight;
And the blood of her veins in the moonlight throbbed to
    her love's refrain.

Tlot-tlot; tlot-tlot!   Had they heard it?   The horse-hoofs
   ringing clear;
Tlot-tlot, tlot-tlot, in the distance?   Were they deaf that
   they did not hear?
Down the ribbon of moonlight, over the brow of the hill,
The highwayman came riding,
            Riding, riding!
The red-coats looked to their priming!   She stood up
   straight and still!

Tlot-tlot, in the frosty silence!   *Tlot-tlot,* in the echoing
   night!
Nearer he came and nearer!   Her face was like a light!
Her eyes grew wide for a moment; she drew one last deep
   breath,
Then her finger moved in the moonlight,
            Her musket shattered the moonlight,
Shattered her breast in the moonlight and warned him —
   with her death.

He turned; he spurred to the West; he did not know who
   stood
Bowed, with her head o'er the musket, drenched with her
   own red blood!
Not till the dawn he heard it, his face grew grey to hear
How Bess, the landlord's daughter,
            The landlord's black-eyed daughter,
Had watched for her love in the moonlight, and died in
   the darkness there.

Back, he spurred like a madman, shrieking a curse to the
   sky,
With the white road smoking behind him and rapier bran-
   dished high!
Blood-red were his spurs i' the golden noon; wine-red was
   his velvet coat,
When they shot him down on the highway,
            Down like a dog on the highway,
And he lay in his blood on the highway, with the bunch
   of lace at his throat.

*   *   *

And still of a winter's night, they say, when the wind is
   in the trees,
When the moon is a ghostly galleon tossed upon cloudy
   seas,
When the road is a ribbon of moonlight over the purple
   moor,
A highwayman comes riding –
         Riding –riding –
A highwayman comes riding, up to the old inn-door.

Over the cobbles he clatters and clangs in the dark inn-
   yard;
He taps with his whip on the shutters, but all is locked
   and barred;
He whistles a tune to the window, and who should be
   waiting there
But the landlord's black-eyed daughter,
         Bess, the landlord's daughter,
Plaiting a dark red love-knot into her long black hair.

ALFRED NOYES

MICHAEL ONDAATJE (1943-　) was born in Ceylon and lived there for eleven years. He attended Dulwich College in England before coming to Canada in 1962. He lives in Toronto, working as teacher, writer and film-maker. His work dwells much upon the bizarre, the extraordinary. He perceives division, constant change and struggle everywhere, even in the domestic world.

Bearhug

Griffin calls to come and kiss him goodnight
I yell ok. Finish something I'm doing,
then something else, walk slowly round
the corner to my son's room.
He is standing arms outstretched
waiting for a bearhug. Grinning.

Why do I give my emotion an animal's name,
give it that dark squeeze of death?
This is the hug which collects
all his small bones and his warm neck against me.
The thin tough body under the pyjamas
locks to me like a magnet of blood.

How long was he standing there
like that, before I came?

MICHAEL ONDAATJE

A House Divided

This midnight breathing
heaves with no sensible rhythm,
is fashioned by no metronome.
Your body, eager
for the extra yard of bed,
reconnoitres and outflanks;
I bend in peculiar angles.
This nightly battle is fought with subtleties:
you get pregnant, I'm sure,
just for extra ground
– immune from kicks now.

Inside you now's another,
thrashing like a fish,
swinging, fighting
for its inch already.

MICHAEL ONDAATJE

WILFRED OWEN (1893-1918) *was born in England, taught for a few years, and was killed at age twenty-five in the First World War, just before the armistice. Friends published his collected poetry,* War and the Pity of War, *after his death. It was edited by Siegfried Sassoon.*

Dulce et Decorum Est

Bent double, like old beggars under sacks,
Knock-kneed, coughing like hags, we cursed through
    sludge,
Till on the haunting flares we turned our backs,
And towards our distant rest began to trudge.
Men marched asleep. Many had lost their boots,
But limped on, blood-shod. All went lame, all blind;
Drunk with fatigue; deaf even to the hoots
Of gas-shells dropping softly behind.

Gas! Gas! Quick, boys! – An ecstasy of fumbling,
Fitting the clumsy helmets just in time,
But someone still was yelling out and stumbling
And floundering like a man in fire or lime. –
Dim through the misty panes and thick green light,
As under a green sea, I saw him drowning.

In all my dreams before my helpless sight
He plunges at me, guttering, choking, drowning.

If in some smothering dreams, you too could pace
Behind the wagon that we flung him in,
And watch the white eyes writhing in his face,
His hanging face, like a devil's sick of sin;
If you could hear, at every jolt, the blood
Come gargling from the froth-corrupted lungs,
Bitter as the cud
Of vile, incurable sores on innocent tongues, –
My friend, you would not tell with such high zest
To children ardent for some desperate glory,
The old Lie: Dulce et decorum est
Pro patria mori.

WILFRED OWEN

*DOROTHY PARKER (1893-1967) was an American journalist,
storywriter and author of light verse that was characteristi-
cally malicious and satirical, a member of the New York
literary group that included Franklin P. Adams. She enjoyed
fame and for long periods in Hollywood a large income.
A great cynic, one of her favourite themes was suicide and
how welcome death would be. She alienated many people as
she grew older, dying alone and of natural causes at the age
of seventy-three.*

Condolence

They hurried here, as soon as you had died,
Their faces damp with haste and sympathy,
And pressed my hand in theirs, and smoothed my knee,
And clicked their tongues, and watched me, mournful-eyed.

Gently they told me of that Other Side –
How, even then, you waited there for me,
And what ecstatic meeting ours would be.
Moved by the lovely tale, they broke, and cried.

And when I smiled, they told me I was brave,
And they rejoiced that I was comforted,
And left, to tell of all the help they gave.
But I had smiled to think how you, the dead,
So curiously preoccupied and grave,
Would laugh, could you have heard the things they said.

DOROTHY PARKER

Résumé

Razors pain you;
Rivers are damp;
Acids stain you;
And drugs cause cramp.
Guns aren't lawful;
Nooses give;
Gas smells awful;
You might as well live.

DOROTHY PARKER

COVENTRY PATMORE (1823-1896): Born in England, Patmore was an assistant in the printed book department of the British Museum. He converted to Roman Catholicism in 1864, and much of his writing deals with religious themes.

The Toys

My little Son, who looked from thoughtful eyes
And moved and spoke in quiet grown-up wise,
Having my law the seventh time disobeyed,
I struck him, and dismissed
With hard words and unkissed,
–His Mother, who was patient, being dead.
Then, fearing lest his grief should hinder sleep,
I visited his bed,
But found him slumbering deep,
With darkened eyelids, and their lashes yet
From his late sobbing wet.
And I, with moan,
Kissing away his tears, left others of my own;
For, on a table drawn beside his head,
He had put, within his reach,
A box of counters and a red-veined stone,
A piece of glass abraded by the beach,
And six or seven shells,
A bottle with bluebells,
And two French copper coins, ranged there with
    careful art,
To comfort his sad heart.
So when that night I prayed
To God, I wept, and said:
"Ah, when at last we lie with trancèd breath,
Not vexing Thee in death,
And Thou rememberest of what toys
We made our joys,
How weakly understood

Thy great commanded good,
Then, fatherly not less
Than I whom Thou hast moulded from the clay,
Thou'lt leave Thy wrath, and say,
'I will be sorry for their childishness.' "

COVENTRY PATMORE.

SHIRLEY I. PAUSTIAN (1916-   ) is a Canadian, born in Saskatchewan and currently living in Alberta. She studied Agriculture and English at the universities of Saskatchewan and Alberta, and has had a varied career as office worker, newspaper reporter, freelance writer and teacher of English in high schools and universities.

Substitute

Quadratic functions
Is what it says at the top of the page.
Except for the sniffles of the boy in the front desk
The room is quiet.
Do you offer grade twelve a Kleenex?

The math teacher left a test.
Equations – yes – but what is a vertex?
And where did a and b come from?
Once I would have known.

No. 69,
Second from the back in the third row,
Squirms and watches me.
He steals a furtive glance at the paper across
   the aisle.
No help there; the blind leads the blind.

The farmer's oats increases in yield by three bushels
   a day,
And the price falls at a prescribed daily rate.
Draw the graph.
When should the farmer sell?
Farm kids would say, suppose it hails? or snows?
What about shelling? Grasshoppers? And who says
That prices will go down?
City kids, these.

The girl in front of 69 moves to one side.
He stretches his neck, peers anxiously, turns back
   a page
And writes.
The kinky-haired kid with the grin is finished.
Can I go now?
Can't you find something useful to do here?
Me? Useful? The grin widens. You gotta be kiddin!
He'll get by.

It's the 69's I worry about.
Stand on your own feet, kid;
Take your licks.
The world forgives the honest grin,
But the shifty eye
Opens no pathways.

SHIRLEY I. PAUSTIAN

For Monnie

I can't find her eyes
they move away
then back again

now she's imitating animals
& insects
and bends over the table
squealing in someone's ear

her friends laugh
but just out of politeness,
they don't like her stupid jokes

she's embarrassing
even dangerous
what if the cops
came into this coffee shop

we'd get busted
because of her
an eighteen-year-old

who's been taking drugs:
pot speed hash acid,
she mixes them together

too bad for us all
that she had a kid
three months ago
and it's in some orphanage

as it is I don't think
she'll last three more months,
everyone in the place is nervous
and looking around

at the other end of the table
Monnie goes on giggling
& making wild faces

MARC PLOURDE (1952-   )

EDGAR ALLAN POE (1809-1849): Born in Boston of actor
parents, Poe was taken into the home of a Richmond merchant
at the age of two. Poe had published his first volume of
poetry by the age of eighteen and was a good scholar, but his
wild habits, particularly drinking and gambling, produced
a break with his guardian. In 1836 he married his fourteen-
year-old cousin and eked out a meagre living as journalist
and editor in Philadelphia and New York. His wife died in
1847 of a lingering illness endured in conditions of great
poverty. Poe lived a further two years. He is perhaps best
known for the morbid imagination displayed in his tales
of horror.

Annabel Lee

It was many and many a year ago,
   In a kingdom by the sea,
That a maiden there lived whom you may know
   By the name of Annabel Lee;
And this maiden she lived with no other thought
   Than to love and be loved by me.

I was a child and she was a child,
   In this kingdom by the sea,
But we loved with a love that was more than love,
   I and my Annabel Lee;
With a love that the winged seraphs of heaven
   Coveted her and me.

And this was the reason that, long ago,
   In this kingdom by the sea,
A wind blew out of a cloud, chilling
   My beautiful Annabel Lee;
So that her highborn kinsmen came
   And bore her away from me,
To shut her up in a sepulchre
   In this kingdom by the sea.

The angels, not half so happy in heaven,
   Went envying her and me;

Yes! that was the reason (as all men know,
    In this kingdom by the sea)
That the wind came out of the cloud by night,
    Chilling and killing my Annabel Lee.

But our love it was stronger by far than the love
    Of those who were older than we,
    Of many far wiser than we;
And neither the angels in heaven above,
    Nor the demons down under the sea,
Can ever dissever my soul from the soul
    Of the beautiful Annabel Lee;
For the moon never beams, without bringing me dreams
    Of the beautiful Annabel Lee:

And the stars never rise, but I feel the bright eyes
    Of the beautiful Annabel Lee;
And so, all the night-tide, I lie down by the side
Of my darling – my darling – my life and my bride,
    In her sepulchre there by the sea,
    In her tomb by the sounding sea.

EDGAR ALLAN POE

*ALEXANDER POPE (1688-1744) was an English poet, a dicta-
tor in the literary world of his time. He made excellent use of
the heroic couplet in his poetry, which was characterized by
biting and malicious wit. He was a hunchback and cripple
as a result of a serious illness in childhood, a circumstance
which, together with his being excluded from the universities
because he was a Catholic, embittered him considerably.
Many of his couplets, such as the first line of the poem
quoted here, have become familiar sayings, often confused
with proverbs.*

A Little Learning

A little learning is a dangerous thing;
Drink deep, or taste not the Pierian spring:
There shallow draughts intoxicate the brain,
And drinking largely sobers us again.
Fired at first sight with what the Muse imparts,
In fearless youth we tempt the heights of Arts;
While from the bounded level of our mind
Short views we take, nor see the lengths behind,
But, more advanced, behold with strange surprise
New distant scenes of endless science rise!
So pleased at first the towering Alps we try,
Mount o'er the vales, and seem to tread the sky;
The eternal snows appear already past,
And the first clouds and mountains seem the last:
But those attained, we tremble to survey
The growing labours of the lengthened way;
The increasing prospect tires our wandering eyes,
Hills peep o'er hills, and Alps on Alps arise!

ALEXANDER POPE

HELEN PORTER (1930-   ) was born in St. John's,
Newfoundland. As well as poetry, she has published short
stories, articles and plays, both in Canada and overseas. She
says of her poetry, "[It] tends to be rather down-to-earth;
I admire the mystical allusions ... of other poets, but don't
do that kind of thing myself."

Housewife

I never thought I'd feel like this
At my age. I thought by this time I'd be
calm and serene,
Occupied by things like gourmet recipes
And refinishing old tables.

Instead of that it's like seventeen again,
March flashes through my flesh as it did then,
Leaving me weak and warm and wondering
What happens next? Will people think I'm strange
With my hair long and straight, though streaking grey?

Why can't I reconcile myself to proper dresses
And hairdos more becoming to my age?
My mother did, and lived in peace
Or did she? I can't believe she ever felt
As I do now, but how would I know really?

My daughters think I'm sensible and solid,
Someone who's always there, to call them in the morning,
To cook the roast, and order pants from Eaton's;
What would they say, I wonder, if I told them
I'd like to go play marbles in the mud?

Or waltz around the kitchen while a country singer
Warbles about falling to pieces; is that what I'm doing?
I never was much of a dancer, although
I always wanted to be. Maybe that
Or something else is what's wrong with me now.

HELEN PORTER

For My Father

I think a time will come when you will understand
That I was forced to try and fly and learn to sing
And that because I fell, echoless, between dark rocks
Is of itself no proof that if I had not run away
I would have grown strong and added to
The long tradition of you and your quiet sires.
Remember too, that this emigrating is of itself
Part of your own long silent heritage.
Else, how sir, did you come to be American?

PAUL POTTS (1911-   )

EZRA POUND (1885-1972): Born in the American Northwest,
Pound left for Europe at age twenty-two as a crusader on
behalf of poetry. He soon became involved with the leading
moderns, including W.B. Yeats and T.S. Eliot. During the
Second World War he broadcast on behalf of the Italian
fascists, but was later ruled mentally unfit to stand trial for
treason. Much of his poetry betrays his wide-ranging and
often erratic intellect.

The River-Merchant's Wife: A Letter

(After Rihaku)

While my hair was still cut straight across my forehead
I played about the front gate, pulling flowers.
You came by on bamboo stilts, playing horse,
You walked about my seat, playing with blue plums.
And we went on living in the village of Chokan:
Two small people, without dislike or suspicion.

At fourteen I married My Lord you.
I never laughed, being bashful.
Lowering my head, I looked at the wall.
Called to, a thousand times, I never looked back.

At fifteen I stopped scowling,
I desired my dust to be mingled with yours
Forever and forever and forever.
Why should I climb the look out?

At sixteen you departed,
You went into far Ku-to-yen, by the river of swirling eddies,
And you have been gone five months.
The monkeys make sorrowful noise overhead.

You dragged your feet when you went out.
By the gate now, the moss is grown, the different mosses,
Too deep to clear them away!
The leaves fall early this autumn, in wind.

The paired butterflies are already yellow with August
Over the grass in the West garden;
They hurt me. I grow older.
If you are coming down through the narrows of the
    river Kiang,
Please let me know beforehand,
And I will come out to meet you
                  As far as Cho-fu-Sa.

EZRA POUND

Salutation

O generation of the thoroughly smug
    and thoroughly uncomfortable,
I have seen fishermen picnicking in the sun,
I have seen them with untidy families,
I have seen their smiles full of teeth
    and heard ungainly laughter.
And I am happier than you are,
And they were happier than I am;
And the fish swim in the lake
    and do not even own clothing.

EZRA POUND

E.J. PRATT (1882-1964) is a Canadian poet, born in New-foundland and educated at St. John's Methodist College. After preaching and teaching at island outposts he went to the University of Toronto where he graduated in philosophy and theology. He taught in the Department of English at the University of Toronto's Victoria College until his retirement in 1953. Much of his poetry has to do with the power of the sea.

Cherries

'I'll never speak to Jamie again'–
Cried Jennie, 'let alone wed,
No, not till blackbirds' wings grow white,
And crab-apple trees grow cherries for spite,
But I'll marry Percy instead.'

But Jamie met her that self-same day,
Where crab-apple trees outspread,
And poured out his heart like a man insane,
And argued until he became profane,
That he never meant what he said.

Now strange as it seems, the truth must be told,
So wildly Jamie pled,
That cherries came out where the crab-apples grew,
And snow-winged blackbirds came down from the blue,
And feasted overhead.

E.J. PRATT

Erosion

It took the sea a thousand years,
A thousand years to trace
The granite features of this cliff,
In crag and scarp and base.

It took the sea an hour one night,
An hour of storm to place
The sculpture of these granite seams
Upon a woman's face.

E.J. PRATT

AL PURDY (1918-   ) was born in Ontario, left school at
sixteen and worked at various jobs. At age twenty-six he
published his first book of poems, but he did not consider
writing for a living until he sold a script to the CBC in 1955.
Of his poetry he once wrote, "I have no one style . . . I can
shift gears like a hot-rod kid. . . I have no ideas about being
a specific kind of poet. I mean, I don't make rules and say
THIS is what a poet HAS to be."

Hockey Players

What they worry about most is injuries
                    broken arms and legs and
fractured skulls opening so doctors
can see such bloody beautiful things
almost not quite happening in the bone rooms
                    as they happen outside –

And the referee?
                    He's right there on the ice
not out of sight among the roaring blue gods
of a game played for passionate businessmen
and a nation of television agnostics
who never agree with the referee and applaud
when he falls flat on his face –

                    On a breakaway
the centre man carrying the puck
his wings trailing a little
                    on both sides why
I've seen the aching glory of a resurrection
                    in their eyes
                    if they score
but crucifixion's agony to lose
– the game?

                We sit up there in the blues
bored and sleepy and suddenly three men
break down the ice in roaring feverish speed and
we stand up in our seats with such a rapid pouring
of delight exploding out of self to join them why

theirs and our orgasm is the rocket stipend
for skating thru the smoky end boards out
of sight and climbing up the appalachian highlands
and racing breast to breast across laurentian barrens
over hudson's diamond bay and down the treeless tundra where
auroras are tubercular and awesome and
stopping isn't feasible or possible or lawful
but we have to and we have to
                              laugh because we must and
stop to look at self and one another but
                    our opponent's never geography
                              or distance why
          it's men
          -just men?

And how do the players feel about it
this combination of ballet and murder?
For years a Canadian specific
to salve the anguish of inferiority
by being good at something the Americans aren't-
And what's the essence of a game like this
which takes a ten year fragment of a man's life
replaced with love that lodges in his brain
              and takes the place of reason?
Besides the fear of injuries
is it the difficulty of ever really overtaking
a hard black rubber disc?

Is it the impatient coach who insists on winning?
Sportswriters friendly but sometimes treacherous?
-And the worrying wives wanting you to quit and
your aching body stretched on the rubbing table
thinking of money in owners' pockets that might be in yours
the butt-slapping camaraderie and the self indulgence
of allowing yourself to be a hero and knowing
everything ends in a pot-belly-

Out on the ice can all these things be forgotten
in swift and skilled delight of speed?
-roaring out the endboards out the city

streets and high up where laconic winds
whisper litanies for a fevered hockey player–
Or racing breast to breast and never stopping
over rooftops of the world and all together
sing the song of winning all together
sing the song of money all together . . .

        (and out in the suburbs
there's the six year old kid
whose reflexes were all wrong
who always fell down and hurt himself and cried
and never learned to skate
          with his friends)–

AL PURDY

My Grandfather Talking –
30 Years Ago

Not now boy not now
some other time I'll tell ya
what it was like
the way it was
without no streets
or names of places here
nothin but moonlight boy
nothin but woods

Why ain't there woods no more?
I lived in the trees an
how far was anywhere was
as far as the trees went
ceptin cities
                    an I never went

They put a road there
where the trees was
an a girl on the road
in a blue dress
an given a place to go
from I went
into the woods with her
it bein the best way
to go an never get there

Walk in the woods an not get lost
wherever the woods go
a house in the way
a wall in the way
a stone in the way
that got there quick as hell
an a man shouting Stop
but you don't dast stop
or everything would fall down

You know it's time boy
when you can't tell anyone
when there ain't none to tell
about whatever it was I was sayin
what I was talkin about
what I was thinkin of – ?

AL PURDY

HENRY REED (1914-   ) is a British writer, better known
for the humorous dramatic pieces he has written for radio than
for his poems. After serving in the army during the Second World
War, he worked as a teacher and finally a broadcaster, journalist,
and radio writer. It is thought by some that his handful of war
poems will be the most enduring of his works.

Naming of Parts

To-day we have naming of parts. Yesterday,
We had daily cleaning. And to-morrow morning,
We shall have what to do after firing. But to-day,
To-day we have naming of parts. Japonica
Glistens like coral in all of the neighbouring gardens,
        and to-day we have naming of parts.

This is the lower sling swivel. And this
Is the upper sling swivel, whose use you will see,
When you are given your slings. And this is the piling swivel,
Which in your case you have not got. The branches
Hold in the gardens their silent, eloquent gestures,
        Which in our case we have not got.

This is the safety-catch, which is always released
With an easy flick of the thumb. And please do not let me
See anyone using his finger. You can do it quite easy
If you have any strength in your thumb. The blossoms
Are fragile and motionless, never letting anyone see
        Any of them using their finger.

And this you can see is the bolt. The purpose of this
Is to open the breech, as you see. We can slide it
Rapidly backwards and forwards: we call this
Easing the spring. And rapidly backwards and forwards
The early bees are assaulting and fumbling the flowers:
        They call it easing the Spring.

They call it easing the Spring: it is perfectly easy
If you have any strength in your thumb: like the bolt,
And the breech, and the cocking-piece, and the point of balance,
Which in our case we have not got; and the almond-blossom
Silent in all of the gardens and the bees going backwards and forwards,
        For to-day we have naming of parts.

HENRY REED

*EDWIN ARLINGTON ROBINSON (1869-1935) was born in
Maine, New England, where he spent an unhappy youth.
His early attempts at publishing his poetry went unrewarded.
Supporting himself by doing various uncongenial jobs, he
paid for the printing of his first published collection. When
the President of the United States, Theodore Roosevelt,
became interested in his work, his luck changed, and he
was eventually able to devote himself to writing. When a
critic wrote that Robinson viewed the world as a prison house,
the poet replied, "The world is not a 'prison house,' but a
kind of spiritual kindergarten where millions of bewildered
infants are trying to spell 'God' with the wrong blocks."*

Miniver Cheevy

Miniver Cheevy, child of scorn,
    Grew lean while he assailed the seasons;
He wept that he was ever born,
    And he had reasons.

Miniver loved the days of old
    When swords were bright and steeds were prancing;
The vision of a warrior bold
    Would set him dancing.

Miniver sighed for what was not,
    And dreamed, and rested from his labors;
He dreamed of Thebes and Camelot,
    And Priam's neighbors.

Miniver mourned the ripe renown
    That made so many a name so fragrant;
He mourned Romance, now on the town,
    And Art, a vagrant.

Miniver loved the Medici,
    Albeit he had never seen one;
He would have sinned incessantly
    Could he have been one.

Miniver cursed the commonplace
    And eyed a khaki suit with loathing;

He missed the medieval grace
   Of iron clothing.

Miniver scorned the gold he sought,
   But sore annoyed was he without it;
Miniver thought, and thought, and thought
   And thought about it.

Miniver Cheevy, born too late,
   Scratched his head and kept on thinking;
Miniver coughed, and called it fate,
   And kept on drinking.

EDWIN ARLINGTON ROBINSON

Richard Cory

Whenever Richard Cory went down town,
  We people on the pavement looked at him:
He was a gentleman from sole to crown,
  Clean favored, and imperially slim.

And he was always quietly arrayed,
  And he was always human when he talked;
But still he fluttered pulses when he said,
  "Good-morning," and he glittered when he walked.

And he was rich–yes, richer than a king,
  And admirably schooled in every grace:
In fine, we thought that he was everything
  To make us wish that we were in his place.

So on we worked, and waited for the light,
  And went without the meat, and cursed the bread;
And Richard Cory, one calm summer night,
  Went home and put a bullet through his head.

EDWIN ARLINGTON ROBINSON

CHRISTINA ROSSETTI (1830-1894) was an English poet of Italian parentage, the daughter of one of a group of exiled painters, literary men and scholars. She served as a model for some Pre-Raphaelite painters. Twice she declined marriage because of her religious scruples. She looked after her mother and devoted herself to religious debate. A serious illness in 1874 left her an invalid.

When I Am Dead

When I am dead, my dearest,
  Sing no sad songs for me;
Plant thou no roses at my head,
  Nor shady cypress tree:
Be the green grass above me
  With showers and dewdrops wet;
And if thou wilt, remember,
  And if thou wilt, forget.

I shall not see the shadows,
  I shall not feel the rain;
I shall not hear the nightingale
  Sing on as if in pain:
And dreaming through the twilight
  That doth not rise nor set,
Haply I may remember,
  And haply may forget.

CHRISTINA ROSSETTI

Who Has Seen the Wind?

Who has seen the wind?
  Neither I nor you;
But when the leaves hang trembling
  The wind is passing thro'.

Who has seen the wind?
  Neither you nor I;
But when the trees bow down their heads
  The wind is passing by.

CHRISTINA ROSSETTI

BUFFY SAINTE-MARIE (1941-   ) is of Cree Indian heritage.
Born in Craven, Saskatchewan, she was adopted by a family
of Micmac Indian descent. She was educated at the University
of Massachusetts, and emerged as a budding actress and
school teacher. She is a poet, songwriter and musician; she
sings, plays the piano and guitar, and writes the music and
lyrics for her own songs. The Universal Soldier *is one of the*
best-known of these.

The Universal Soldier

He's five foot two and he's six feet four,
  he fights with missiles and with spears,
He's all of thirty-one and he's only seventeen,
  he's been a soldier for a thousand years.

He's a Catholic, a Hindu, an Atheist, a Jain,
  a Buddhist and a Baptist and a Jew,
And he knows he shouldn't kill and he knows he always will
  kill you for me, my friend, and me for you;

And he's fighting for Canada, he's fighting for France,
  he's fighting for the U.S.A.,
And he's fighting for the Russians and he's fighting for Japan,
  and he thinks we'll put an end to war that way.

And he's fighting for democracy, he's fighting for the Reds,
  he says it's for the peace of all,
He's the one who must decide who's to live and who's to die,
  and he never sees the writing on the wall.

But without him how would Hitler have condemned him
                                     at Dachau
  without him Caesar would have stood alone.
He's the one who gives his body as a weapon of the war,
  and without him all this killing can't go on.

He's the Universal Soldier and he really is to blame,
  his orders come from far away no more,
They come from him and you and me, and, brothers can't you see,
  This is not the way we put an end to war.

BUFFY SAINTE-MARIE

CARL SANDBURG (1878-1967) was an American poet and
journalist of Swedish ancestry. He worked his way through
college doing odd jobs, travelled as a hobo in the west, served
in the Spanish-American war, and worked in advertising.
He then turned to journalism, and eventually became an
editorial writer for the Chicago Daily News. After his
marriage in 1908 he began to write more and more poetry,
winning two national awards by 1920. He was much influ-
enced by Whitman in his poetry, which deals with American
life in all its forms.

I Am the People, the Mob

I am the people – the mob – the crowd – the mass.
Do you know that all the great work of the world
          is done through me?
I am the workingman, the inventor, the maker of
          the world's food and clothes.
I am the audience that witnesses history. The
          Napoleons come from me and the Lincolns.
          They die. And then I send forth more Napo-
          leons and Lincolns.
I am the seed ground. I am a prairie that will stand
          for much plowing. Terrible storms pass over
          me. I forget. The best of me is sucked out and
          wasted. I forget. Everything but Death comes
          to me and makes me work and give up what
          I have. And I forget.
Sometimes I growl, shake myself and spatter a few
          red drops for history to remember. Then –
          I forget.
When I, the People, learn to remember, when I,
          the People, use the lessons of yesterday and
          no longer forget who robbed me last year,
          who played me for a fool – then there will be

no speaker in the world say the name: "The
People," with any fleck of a sneer in his voice
or any far-off smile of derision.
The mob–the crowd–the mass–will arrive
then.

CARL SANDBURG

Soup

I saw a famous man eating soup.
I say he was lifting a fat broth
Into his mouth with a spoon.
His name was in the newspapers that day
Spelled out in tall black headlines
And thousands of people were talking about him.

When I saw him,
He sat bending his head over a plate
Putting soup in his mouth with a spoon.

CARL SANDBURG

Fog

The fog comes
on little cat feet.
It sits looking
over harbor and city
on silent haunches
and then moves on.

CARL SANDBURG

*SIEGFRIED SASSOON (1886-1967) was of Anglo-Jewish ances-
try, known for his poetry exposing the horror of war and
satirizing the English upper classes. He served for a year and
a half in the First World War, won a Military Cross, declared
himself a pacifist, threw his Military Cross into the sea and
refused to fight. He was judged insane, sent to a sanatorium,
and later returned to active duty. He was a friend of Wilfred
Owen. A poet from his university days, he was a modest man
with a great faculty for laughter.*

Everyone Sang

*Everyone suddenly burst out singing;
And I was filled with such delight
As prisoned birds must find in freedom
Winging wildly across the white
Orchards and dark-green fields; on; on; and out
    of sight.*

*Everyone's voice was suddenly lifted,
And beauty came like the setting sun.
My heart was shaken with tears; and horror
Drifted away . . . O but every one
Was a bird; and the song was wordless; the
    singing will never be done.*

SIEGFRIED SASSOON.

F.R. SCOTT (1899-   ) was born in Quebec City and studied law at McGill University. In 1928 he joined the staff at McGill, eventually becoming Dean of Law in the four years prior to his retirement in 1964. He has received much acclaim for his achievements in the arts, humanities and social sciences. He was an ardent defender of civil liberties and social justice, and much of his verse criticizes Canadian society.

Examiner

The routine trickery of the examination
Baffles these hot and discouraged youths.
Driven by they know not what external pressure
They pour their hated self-analysis
Through the nib of confession, onto the accusatory page.

I, who have plotted their immediate downfall,
I am entrusted with the divine categories,
ABCD and the hell of E,
The parade of prize and the backdoor of pass.

In the tight silence
Standing by a green window
Watching the fertile earth graduate its sons
with more compassion – not commanding the shape
Of stem and stamen, bringing the trees to pass
By shift of sunlight and increase of rain,
For each seed the whole soil, for the inner life
The environment receptive and contributory –
I shudder at the narrow frames of our text-book schools
In which we plant our so various seedlings.

Each brick-walled barracks
Cut into numbered rooms, black-boarded,
Ties the venturing shoot to the master stick;
The screw-desk rows of lads and girls
subdued in the shade of an adult –
Their acid subsoil –
Shape the new to the old in the ashen garden.

Shall we open the whole skylight of thought
To those tiptoe minds, bring them our frontier worlds
And the boundless uplands of art for their field of growth?
Or shall we pass them the chosen poems with the foot-notes,
Ring the bell on their thoughts, period their play,
Make laws for averages and plans for means,
Print one history book for a whole province, and
Let ninety thousand read page 10 by Tuesday?

As I gather the inadequate paper evidence, I hear
Across the neat campus lawn
The professional mowers drone, clipping the inch-high green.

F.R. SCOTT

ROBERT SERVICE (1874-1958) was born in England, the "lust for adventure" eventually taking him to Canada. For seven years he travelled and worked at numerous occupations, finally finding employment with the Canadian Bank of Commerce in the Yukon. Here, influenced by Rudyard Kipling, he started to write, and was surprised that his work was accepted. He served in the First World War and settled in France. His "blood and guts style" of poetry shows he had no great pretensions as a poet, though his popularity is considerable.

The Shooting of Dan McGrew

A bunch of the boys were whooping it up in the
    Malamute saloon;
The kid that handles the music-box was hitting a rag-time
    tune;
Back of the bar, in a solo game, sat Dangerous Dan
    McGrew,
And watching his luck was his light-o'-love, the lady
    that's known as Lou.

When out of the night, which was fifty below, and into
    the din and the glare,
There stumbled a miner fresh from the creeks, dog-dirty,
    and loaded for bear.
He looked like a man with a foot in the grave and
    scarcely the strength of a louse,
Yet he tilted a poke of dust on the bar, and he called for
    drinks on the house.
There was none could place the stranger's face, though
    we searched ourselves for a clue;
But we drank his health, and the last to drink was
    Dangerous Dan McGrew.

There's men that somehow just grip your eyes, and hold
    them hard like a spell;
And such was he, and he looked to me like a man who
    had lived in hell;
With a face most hair, and the dreary stare of a dog
    whose day is done,

As he watered the green stuff in his glass, and the drops
    fell one by one.
Then I got to figgering who he was, and wondering what
    he'd do,
And I turned my head – and there watching him was the
    lady that's known as Lou.

His eyes went rubbering round the room, and he seemed
    in a kind of daze,
Till at last that old piano fell in the way of his wandering
    gaze.
The rag-time kid was having a drink; there was no one
    else on the stool,
So the stranger stumbles across the room, and flops
    down there like a fool.

In a buckskin shirt that was glazed with dirt he sat, and
   I saw him sway;
Then he clutched the keys with his talon hands – my God!
   but that man could play.

Were you ever out in the Great Alone, when the moon
   was awful clear,
And the icy mountains hemmed you in with a silence
   you most could hear;
With only the howl of a timber wolf, and you camped
   there in the cold,
A half-dead thing in a stark, dead world, clean mad for
   the muck called gold;
While high overhead, green, yellow and red, the North
   Lights swept in bars? –
Then you've a hunch what the music meant . . . hunger
   and night and the stars.

And hunger not of the belly kind, that's banished with
   bacon and beans,
But the gnawing hunger of lonely men for a home and all
   that it means;
For a fireside far from the cares that are, four walls and
   a roof above;
But oh! so cramful of cosy joy, and crowned with a
   woman's love –
A woman dearer than all the world, and true as Heaven
   is true –
(God! how ghastly she looks through her rouge, – the lady
   that's known as Lou.)

Then on a sudden the music changed, so soft that you
   scarce could hear;
But you felt that your life had been looted clean of all
   that it once held dear;
That someone had stolen the woman you loved; that her
   love was a devil's lie;
That your guts were gone, and the best for you was to
   crawl away and die.
'Twas the crowning cry of a heart's despair, and it thrilled
   you through and through –
"I guess I'll make it a spread misere," said Dangerous
   Dan McGrew.

The music almost died away . . . then it burst like a pent-
  up flood;
And it seemed to say, "Repay, repay," and my eyes were
  blind with blood.
The thought came back of an ancient wrong, and it stung
  like a frozen lash,
And the lust awoke to kill, to kill . . . then the music
  stopped with a crash,
And the stranger turned, and his eyes they burned
  in a most peculiar way;
In a buckskin shirt that was glazed with dirt he sat, and
  I saw him sway;
Then his lips went in in a kind of grin, and he spoke, and
  his voice was calm,
And "Boys," says he, "you don't know me, and none of
  you care a damn;
But I want to state, and my words are straight, and I'll bet
  my poke they're true,
That one of you is a hound of hell . . . and that one is
  Dan McGrew."

Then I ducked my head, and the lights went out, and two
  guns blazed in the dark,
And a woman screamed, and the lights went up, and two
  men lay stiff and stark.
Pitched on his head, and pumped full of lead, was
  Dangerous Dan McGrew,
While the man from the creeks lay clutched to the breast
  of the lady that's known as Lou.

These are the simple facts of the case, and I guess I ought
  to know.
They say that the stranger was crazed with "hooch," and
  I'm not denying it's so.
I'm not so wise as the lawyer guys, but strictly between
  us two—
The woman that kissed him and — pinched his
  poke — was the lady that's known as Lou.

ROBERT SERVICE

WILLIAM SHAKESPEARE (1564-1616) is the most famous writer in all English literature. Born at Stratford-on-Avon, he probably attended the local grammar school. He was married at age eighteen. It is not known when he went to London and became involved with the theatre–actors and playwrights in those days were low on the social scale and little was recorded of their lives. His plays and poetry were certainly acclaimed in his own time, but it was not until the 19th century that the "worship" of Shakespeare began, and perhaps went too far. His work is remarkable for its poetic excellence and profound insight into human character.

Let Me Not to the Marriage of True Minds

Let me not to the marriage of true minds
Admit impediments. Love is not love
Which alters when it alteration finds,
Or bends with the remover to remove:
O no! it is an ever-fixèd mark
That looks on tempests, and is never shaken;
It is the star to every wandering bark,
Whose worth's unknown, although his height be taken.
Love's not Time's fool, though rosy lips and cheeks

Within his bending sickle's compass come;
Love alters not with his brief hours and weeks,
But beats it out ev'n to the edge of doom.
  If this be error, and upon me proved,
  I never writ, nor no man ever loved.

WILLIAM SHAKESPEARE

The Seven Ages of Man

                        All the world's a stage,
And all the men and women merely players.
They have their exits and their entrances;
And one man in his time plays many parts,
His acts being seven ages. At first the infant,
Mewling and puking in the nurse's arms.
And then the whining school-boy, with his satchel,
And shining morning face, creeping like snail
Unwillingly to school. And then the lover,
Sighing like furnace, with a woful ballad
Made to his mistress' eyebrow. Then a soldier,
Full of strange oaths, and bearded like the pard,
Jealous in honour, sudden and quick in quarrel,
Seeking the bubble reputation
Even in the cannon's mouth. And then the justice,
In fair round belly with good capon lin'd,
With eyes severe, and beard of formal cut,
Full of wise saws and modern instances;
And so he plays his part. The sixth age shifts
Into the lean and slipper'd pantaloon,
With spectacles on nose and pouch on side,
His youthful hose well sav'd a world too wide
For his shrunk shank; and his big manly voice,
Turning again toward childish treble, pipes
And whistles in his sound. Last scene of all,
That ends this strange eventful history,
Is second childishness and mere oblivion,
Sans teeth, sans eyes, sans taste, sans everything.

WILLIAM SHAKESPEARE,
(from *As You Like It* Act II Sc VII).

Who Loves the Rain

Who loves the rain,
And loves his home,
And looks on life with quiet eyes,
   Him will I follow through the storm;
   And at his hearth-fire keep me warm;
Nor hell nor heaven shall that soul surprise,
   Who loves the rain,
   And loves his home,
And looks on life with quiet eyes.

FRANCIS SHAW

*PERCY BYSSHE SHELLEY (1792-1822) was an English Roman-
tic poet noted for the sensitivity of his lyrics, the vividness of
his imagery and imagination, his belief in the perfectability
of mankind, and his rebellion against all authority. Through-
out his life he was childlike and amoral. He was married
twice and left England heartbroken when his two children
were taken from his custody. He was drowned at age thirty
during a storm in the Adriatic.*

Ozymandias

I met a traveller from an antique land
   Who said: Two vast and trunkless legs of stone
Stand in the desert. Near them on the sand,
   Half sunk, a shatter'd visage lies, whose frown

And wrinkled lip and sneer of cold command
   Tell that its sculptor well those passions read
Which yet survive, stamp'd on these lifeless things,
   The hand that mock'd them and the heart that fed;

   And on the pedestal these words appear:
'My name is Ozymandias, king of kings:
   Look on my works, ye Mighty, and despair!'

Nothing beside remains. Round the decay
   Of that colossal wreck, boundless and bare,
The lone and level sands stretch far away.

P. B. SHELLEY

EDWARD ROWLAND SILL (1841-1887) was an American writer of wide culture and high ideals. He worked in law and journalism, and as a professor of English at the University of California. His health was frail. One of his best-known poems is the one that appears here.

Opportunity

This I beheld, or dreamed it in a dream:
There spread a cloud of dust along a plain;
And underneath the cloud, or in it, raged
A furious battle, and men yelled, and swords
Shocked upon swords and shields. A prince's banner
Wavered, then staggered backward, hemmed by foes.
A craven hung along the battle's edge,
And thought, "Had I a sword of keener steel –
That blue blade that the king's son bears, – but this
Blunt thing –!" he snapped and flung it from his hand,
And lowering crept away and left the field.
Then came the king's son, wounded, sore bested,
And weaponless, and saw the broken sword,
Hilt-buried in the dry and trodden sand,
And ran and snatched it, and with battle-shout
Lifted afresh he hewed his enemy down,
And saved a great cause that heroic day.

EDWARD ROWLAND SILL

No Respect

I have no respect for you
For you would not tell the truth about your grief
But laughed at it
When the first pang was past
And made it a thing of nothing.
You said
That what had been
Had never been
That what was
Was not:
You have a light mind
And a coward's soul.

STEVIE SMITH (1908-1971)

RICHARD SOMMER (1934-   ) was born and raised in Minnesota, worked as an electric meter reader and dance company stage manager, attended Harvard University, and went to Montreal in 1962 to teach literature. About poetry he says, "[It] will persist or re-emerge in any society because (some) human beings will always have to make it."

The Fisherman

Still there is a photograph of me
crouched against the railings of a bridge
watching my father make a mess of casting
a brilliant fly into the bushes.

My father tried fly-fishing because all
the men who were good at it smoked pipes.

My father smoked a pipe because the men
who liked pipes were good at fly-casting.

I remember the thrust of my face against
the cool railings, tilted down at the stream
or drawn back, watching my father.

I remember also that my father didn't
catch anything although his tacklebox
had everything already in it.

If my father were still living, I think
I would take him in my arms and kiss him
and tell him that it didn't matter.

But that is easier to say because
he is dead and I don't have to do it.

I still don't know who took the picture
of the railings, of me, of my father's legs.

It probably wasn't my mother.

RICHARD SOMMER

RAYMOND SOUSTER (1921-   ): Born in Toronto, Souster
served with the airforce in the Second World War, and has
been associated with several literary magazines. He is
employed by the Bank of Commerce, and has written several
poems about his native city. Souster comments, "Whoever
I write to, I want to make the substance of the poem so
immediate, so real, so clear, that the reader feels the same
exhilaration – be it fear or joy – that I derived from the
experience that triggered the poem in the first place."

Evening in the Suburbs

Around six he arrives
from a hard day at the office
His dog greets him
his children greet him
even his wife greets him
He sits down
his wife sits down
his children sit down
even his dog sits down
and they eat supper
Then he lights his cigar
reads the evening paper
the sports page
the markets the comics
Gets up
goes into the garden
where he adjusts the sprinkler
turns the water on
sits down again
watching the drops
fall through the air
and goes to sleep
in the deck-chair
When he wakes up
it's dark outside

the sprinkler's off
He lights a cigar
and goes inside
the house is empty
the lights are out
then he remembers
his wife's at the church
his children next door
watching TV
even his dog's gone
He takes a beer
from the refrigerator
but the beer doesn't taste right
he sits down again
in his easy chair
picks up the paper
but his eyes are tired
he doesn't feel like reading
Still he feels like doing something
and he takes the paper
and rips it down the middle
he goes to the kitchen
and takes the beer bottle
and throws it through the window
his dog coming from the cellar
gets booted in the rear
Then he feels better
he feels good again
sits down in his chair
falls asleep like a child.

RAYMOND SOUSTER

The Introduction

My first introduction to poetry:
our form master on the blackboard
breaking up one of the stanzas
from Wilfred Campbell's "August Reverie"
into principal and subordinate clauses.

RAYMOND SOUSTER

Lake of Bays

"Well, I'm not chicken . . ."
that skinny ten-year old girl
balanced on the crazy-high railing
of the Dorset bridge:

                      suddenly let go
down
fifty feet into the water.

"That one will never grow up
to be a lady," my mother said
as we walked away.

but I'll remember
her brown body dropping like a stone
long after I've forgotten
many many ladies . . .

RAYMOND SOUSTER

ROBERT SOUTHEY (1774-1843) was an English poet of the
Romantic movement. He was expelled from school for an
essay he wrote against the practice of flogging at the school.
He went on to Oxford University, married, travelled in Europe,
and wrote a great deal of verse and prose. His longer poems
are little read now, though they were much admired during
his lifetime. He preceded Wordsworth as Poet Laureate of
England.

After Blenheim

It was a summer evening,
　　Old Kaspar's work was done,
And he before his cottage door
　　Was sitting in the sun;
And by him sported on the green
His little grandchild Wilhelmine.

She saw her brother Peterkin
　　Roll something large and round
Which he beside the rivulet
　　In playing there had found;
He came to ask what he had found
That was so large and smooth and round.

Old Kaspar took it from the boy
　　Who stood expectant by;
And then the old man shook his head,
　　And with a natural sigh
''Tis some poor fellow's skull,' said he,
'Who fell in the great victory.

'I find them in the garden,
　　For there's many here about;
And often when I go to plough
　　The ploughshare turns them out.
For many thousand men,' said he,
'Were slain in that great victory.'

'Now tell us what 'twas all about,'
　　Young Peterkin he cries;

And little Wilhelmine looks up
  With wonder-waiting eyes;
'Now tell us all about the war,
And what they fought each other for.'

'It was the English,' Kaspar cried,
  'Who put the French to rout;
But what they fought each other for
  I could not well make out.
But everybody said,' quoth he,
'That 'twas a famous victory.

'My father lived at Blenheim then,
  Yon little stream hard by;
They burnt his dwelling to the ground,
  And he was forced to fly:
So with his wife and child he fled,
Nor had he where to rest his head.

'With fire and sword the country round
  Was wasted far and wide,
And many a childing mother then
  And new-born baby died:
But things like that, you know, must be
At every famous victory.

'They say it was a shocking sight
  After the field was won;
For many thousand bodies here
  Lay rotting in the sun:
But things like that, you know, must be
After a famous victory.

'Great praise the Duke of Marlbro' won
  And our good Prince Eugene;'
'Why, 'twas a very wicked thing!'
  Said little Wilhelmine;
'Nay . . nay . . my little girl,' quoth he,
'It was a famous victory.

'And everybody praised the Duke
  Who this great fight did win.'

'But what good came of it at last?'
    Quoth little Peterkin: –
'Why, that I cannot tell,' said he,
'But 'twas a famous victory.'

ROBERT SOUTHEY

The Inchcape Rock

No stir in the air, no stir in the sea,
The ship was as still as she could be;
Her sails from heaven received no motion,
Her keel was steady in the ocean.

Without either sign or sound of their shock,
The waves flowed over the Inchcape Rock;
So little they rose, so little they fell,
They did not move the Inchcape Bell.

The pious Abbot of Aberbrothock
Had placed that bell on the Inchcape Rock;
On a buoy in the storm it floated and swung,
And over the waves its warning rung.

When the Rock was hid by the surge's swell,
The mariners heard the warning bell;
And then they knew the perilous Rock,
And blessed the Abbot of Aberbrothock.

The sun in heaven was shining gay;
All things were joyful on that day;
The sea-birds screamed as they wheeled round,
And there was joyance in their sound.

The buoy of the Inchcape Bell was seen,
A darker speck on the ocean green;

Sir Ralph the Rover walked his deck,
And fixed his eye on the darker speck.

He felt the cheering power of spring;
It made him whistle, it made him sing:
His heart was mirthful to excess,
But the Rover's mirth was wickedness.

His eye was on the Inchcape float;
Quoth he: "My men, put out the boat,
And row me to the Inchcape Rock,
And I'll plague the Abbot of Aberbrothock."

The boat is lowered, the boatmen row,
And to the Inchcape Rock they go;
Sir Ralph bent over from his boat,
And he cut the bell from the Inchcape float.

Down sank the bell with a gurgling sound,
The bubbles rose and burst around;
Quoth Sir Ralph: "The next who comes to the Rock
Won't bless the Abbot of Aberbrothock."

Sir Ralph the Rover sailed away;
He scoured the seas for many a day;
And now, grown rich with plundered store,
He steers his course for Scotland's shore.

So thick a haze o'erspreads the sky
They cannot see the sun on high;
The wind hath blown a gale all day,
At evening it hath died away.

On the deck the Rover takes his stand;
So dark it is, they see no land.
Quoth Sir Ralph: "It will be lighter soon,
For there is the dawn of the rising moon."

"Canst hear," said one, "the breakers roar?
For methinks we should be near the shore."
"Now where we are I cannot tell,
But I wish we could hear the Inchcape Bell."

They heard no sound; the swell is strong;
Though the wind has fallen, they drift along,
Till the vessel strikes with a shivering shock;
Cried they: "It is the Inchcape Rock!"

Sir Ralph the Rover tore his hair,
He cursed himself in his despair:
The waves rush in on every side;
The ship is sinking beneath the tide.

But, even in his dying fear,
One dreadful sound could the Rover hear, –
A sound as if, with the Inchcape Bell,
The fiends below were ringing his knell.

ROBERT SOUTHEY

My Parents Kept Me

My parents kept me from children who were rough
Who threw words like stones and who wore torn clothes.
Their thighs showed through rags. They ran in the street
And climbed cliffs and stripped by the country streams.

I feared more than tigers their muscles like iron
Their jerking hands and their knees tight on my arms.
I feared the salt coarse pointing of those boys
Who copied my lisp behind me on the road.

They were lithe, they sprang out behind hedges
Like dogs to bark at my world. They threw mud
While I looked the other way, pretending to smile.
I longed to forgive them, but they never smiled.

STEPHEN SPENDER (1909-   )

*SIR JOHN SUCKLING (1609-1642) was born in Norfolk,
England, of a wealthy family. He lived at the court in
London and was a leader of the Royalist party during the
early days of the troubles leading to England's Civil War.
He eventually fled to Paris and is said to have committed
suicide there. His plays and poems are remembered for their
good lyrics and their wit.*

The Constant Lover

Out upon it, I have lov'd
   Three whole days together;
And am like to love three more,
   If it prove fair weather.

Time shall molt away his wings
   Ere he shall discover
In the whole wide world again
   Such a constant lover.

But the spite on't is, no praise
   Is due at all to me:
Love with me had made no stays
   Had it any been but she.

Had it any been but she
   And that very face,
There had been at least ere this
   A dozen dozen in her place.

SIR JOHN SUCKLING

Why So Pale and Wan

Why so pale and wan, fond lover?
    Prithee, why so pale?
Will, when looking well can't move her,
    Looking ill prevail?
    Prithee, why so pale?

Why so dull and mute, young sinner?
    Prithee, why so mute?
Will, when speaking well can't win her,
    Saying nothing do't?
    Prithee, why so mute?

Quit, quit for shame! This will not move;
    This cannot take her.
If of herself she will not love,
    Nothing can make her:
    The devil take her!

SIR JOHN SUCKLING

MAY SWENSON (1919-   ) was born in Utah and now lives in New York. Poet, playwright, literary critic and translator, she says, "I devise my own forms. My themes are from the organic, the inorganic, and the psychological world."

Southbound on the Freeway

A tourist came in from Orbitville,
parked in the air, and said:

The creatures of this star
are made of metal and glass.

Through the transparent parts
you can see their guts.

Their feet are round and roll
on diagrams or long

measuring tapes, dark
with white lines.

They have four eyes.
The two in back are red.

Sometimes you can see a five-eyed
one, with a red eye turning

on the top of his head.
He must be special –

the others respect him
and go slow

when he passes, winding
among them from behind.

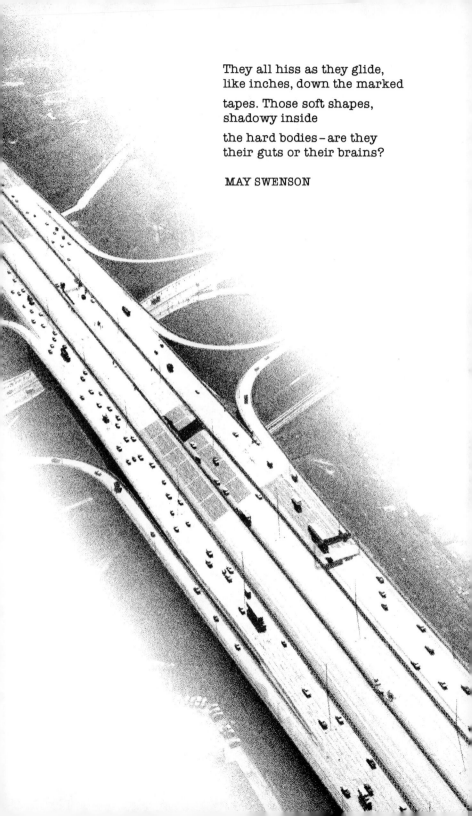

They all hiss as they glide,
like inches, down the marked

tapes. Those soft shapes,
shadowy inside

the hard bodies – are they
their guts or their brains?

MAY SWENSON

In My Host's Garden

"Don't break it!" he said,
   then broke off and gave me
   a branch of his plum.

TAIKI (d. 1771)

ALFRED, LORD TENNYSON (1809-1892) is probably the poet who best represents the Victorian era in England. His poems are melodious and show great craftsmanship, though they are sometimes criticized for artificiality of style. They attracted a large audience. He once said, "I is not always the author speaking of himself, but the voice of the human race speaking through him."

As Thro' the Land at Eve We Went

As thro' the land at eve we went,
   And pluck'd the ripen'd ears,
We fell out, my wife and I,
We fell out, I know not why,
   And kiss'd again with tears.
And blessings on the falling out
   That all the more endears
When we fall out with those we love
   And kiss again with tears!
For when we came where lies the child
   We lost in other years,
There above the little grave,
O there above the little grave,
   We kiss'd again with tears.

ALFRED, LORD TENNYSON

CHARLES HANSON TOWNE (1877-1949) was an American writer and columnist, at one time editor of Harper's Bazaar. *"To be an editor, and a writer – that was my earliest dream,"* *he once said, "and never once did I waver from my purpose."*

Of One Self-Slain

When he went blundering back to God,
   His songs half written, his work half done,
Who knows what paths his bruised feet trod,
   What hills of peace or pain he won?

I hope God smiled, and took his hand,
   And said, "Poor truant, passionate fool!
Life's book is hard to understand –
   Why couldst thou not remain at school?"

CHARLES HANSON TOWNE

JOHN UPDIKE (1932-   ) was born in Pennsylvania and educated in fine arts at Harvard and Oxford. He was once a staff reporter for New Yorker. *As a poet, he began as a writer of light verse, and his later poetry maintains a liveliness. He has written several novels, and is better known as a novelist.*

Ex-Basketball Player

Pearl Avenue runs past the high-school lot,
Bends with the trolley tracks, and stops, cut off
Before it has a chance to go two blocks,
At Colonel McComsky Plaza. Berth's Garage
Is on the corner facing west, and there,
Most days, you'll find Flick Webb, who helps Berth out.

Flick stands tall among the idiot pumps –
Five on a side, the old bubble-head style,
Their rubber elbows hanging loose and low.
One's nostrils are two S's, and his eyes
An E and O. And one is squat, without
A head at all – more of a football type.

Once Flick played for the high-school team, the Wizards.
He was good: in fact, the best. In '46
He bucketed three hundred ninety points,
A county record still. The ball loved Flick.
I saw him rack up thirty-eight or forty
In one home game. His hands were like wild birds.

He never learned a trade, he just sells gas,
Checks oil, and changes flats. Once in a while,
As a gag, he dribbles an inner tube,
But most of us remember anyway.
His hands are fine and nervous on the lug wrench.
It makes no difference to the lug wrench, though.

Off work, he hangs around Mae's Luncheonette.
Grease-grey and kind of coiled, he plays pinball,
Sips lemon cokes, and smokes those thin cigars;
Flick seldom speaks to Mae, just sits and nods
Beyond her face towards bright applauding tiers
Of Necco Wafers, Nibs, and Juju Beads.

JOHN UPDIKE

Superman

I drive my car to supermarket,
  The way I take is superhigh,
A superlot is where I park it,
  And Super Suds are what I buy.

Supersalesmen sell me tonic –
  Super-Tone-O, for Relief.
The planes I ride are supersonic.
  In trains, I like the Super Chief.

Supercilious men and women
  Call me superficial – *me*,
Who so superbly learned to swim in
  Supercolossality.

Superphosphate-fed foods feed me;
  Superservice keeps me new.
Who would dare to supersede me,
  Super-super-superwho?

JOHN UPDIKE

*MIRIAM WADDINGTON (1917-   ) was born in Winnipeg
and educated at the Universities of Toronto and Pennsylvania.
She has been a social worker in Montreal, and a member of
the English department at York University. About her poetry
she says the key to it is language: "My Canadian English
takes its cue from the prairies where I was born and con-
ceals more than it reveals."*

The Hockey Players

Stiff as flowers
lined up beside park benches
the child hockey-players
parade their colours;
under the heavy helmets
their eyes weave a garland
of constant wonder.

Who has planted them
in the forest of winter
so far from their childhood?
Who are those giant spectators
who chopped down the summer
and now fill the arena
with loud expectation?

MIRIAM WADDINGTON

Earth

"A planet doesn't explode of itself," said drily
The Martian astronomer, gazing off into the air –
"That they were able to do it is proof that highly
intelligent beings must have been living there."

JOHN HALL WHEELOCK (1886-1978)

*WALT WHITMAN (1819-1892) was an American poet whose
work greatly influenced many other poets. He had little for-
mal education. In his youth he lived a Bohemian life, and he
taught school, did newspaper work, and became an army
nurse during the Civil War. His poetry was attacked when it
first appeared, being new in thought and style. He celebrated
life, America, democracy, and the common man, and was
very much against the romantic love-poets, who, he said,
were "forever occupied in dyspeptic amours with dyspeptic
women."*

Animals

I think I could turn and live with animals, they are so
    placid and self-contained;
I stand and look at them long and long.
They do not sweat and whine about their condition;
They do not lie awake in the dark and weep for their sins;
They do not make me sick, discussing their duty to God;
Not one is dissatisfied – not one is demented with the mania
    of owning things;
Not one kneels to another, nor to his kind that lived
    thousands of years ago;
Not one is respectable or industrious over the whole earth.

WALT WHITMAN
(from *Song of Myself*)

Miracles

Why, who makes much of a miracle?
As to me I know of nothing else but miracles,
Whether I walk the streets of Manhattan,
Or dart my sights over the roofs of houses toward the sky,
Or wade with naked feet along the beach just in the edge
    of the water,
Or stand under trees in the woods,
Or sit at table at dinner with the rest,
Or look at strangers opposite me riding in the car,
Or watch honey-bees busy around the hive of a summer
    forenoon,
Or animals feeding in the fields,
Or birds, or the wonderfulness of insects in the air,
Or the wonderfulness of the sundown, or the stars shining
    so quiet and bright,
Or the exquisite delicate thin curve of the new moon in
    spring;
These with the rest, one and all, are to me miracles,
The whole referring, yet each distinct and in its place.

To me every hour of the light and dark is a miracle,
Every cubic inch of space is a miracle,
Every square yard of the surface of the earth is spread
    with the same,
Every foot of the interior swarms with the same.

To me the sea is a continual miracle,
The fishes that swim – the rocks – the motion of the waves –
    the ships with men in them,
What stranger miracles are there?

WALT WHITMAN

WILLIAM WORDSWORTH (1770-1850) was an early leader of
the English Romantic Movement. Orphaned at age thirteen,
he was educated by an uncle, and later at Cambridge.
His stay in France saw him involved enthusiastically with
the French Revolution. The rest of his life he spent mostly
in England's Lake District, able to devote himself to writing
because of various legacies. His poetry shows his love of
nature and his humanitarianism. His revolutionary ardour
eventually cooled sufficiently for him to be made Poet Laureate
of England in 1843.

Lucy Gray

Oft' I had heard of Lucy Gray:
And, when I crossed the wild,
I chanced to see at break of day
The solitary child.

No mate, no comrade Lucy knew;
She dwelt on a wide moor,
– The sweetest thing that ever grew
Beside a human door!

You yet may spy the fawn at play,
The hare upon the green;
But the sweet face of Lucy Gray
Will never more be seen.

"To-night will be a stormy night –
You to the town must go;
And take a lantern, Child, to light
Your mother through the snow."

"That, Father! will I gladly do:
'Tis scarcely afternoon –
The minster-clock has just struck two,
And yonder is the moon!"

At this the Father raised his hook,
And snapped a faggot-band;
He plied his work; – and Lucy took
The lantern in her hand.

Not blither is the mountain roe:
With many a wanton stroke
Her feet disperse the powdery snow,
That rises up like smoke.

The storm came on before its time:
She wandered up and down;
And many a hill did Lucy climb:
But never reached the town.

The wretched parents all that night
Went shouting far and wide;
But there was neither sound nor sight
To serve them for a guide.

At day-break on a hill they stood
That overlooked the moor;
And thence they saw the bridge of wood
A furlong from their door.

They wept – and, turning homeward, cried,
"In heaven we all shall meet;"
– When in the snow the mother spied
The print of Lucy's feet.

Then downwards from the steep hill's edge
They tracked the footmarks small;
And through the broken hawthorn hedge,
And by the long stone-wall;

And then an open field they crossed;
The marks were still the same;
They tracked them on, nor ever lost;
And to the bridge they came.

They followed from the snowy bank
Those footmarks, one by one,
Into the middle of the plank;
And further there were none!

– Yet some maintain that to this day
She is a living child;
That you may see sweet Lucy Gray
Upon the lonesome wild.

O'er rough and smooth she trips along,
And never looks behind;
And sings a solitary song
That whistles in the wind.

WILLIAM WORDSWORTH

Pretty Words

Poets make pets of pretty, docile words:
I love smooth words, like gold-enameled fish
Which circle slowly with a silken swish,
And tender ones, like downy-feathered birds:
Words shy and dappled, deep-eyed deer in herds,
Come to my hand, and playful if I wish,
Or purring softly at a silver dish,
Blue Persian kittens, fed on cream and curds.

I love bright words, words up and singing early;
Words that are luminous in the dark, and sing;
Warm lazy words, white cattle under trees;
I love words opalescent, cool, and pearly,
Like midsummer moths, and honied words like bees,
Gilded and sticky, with a little sting.

ELINOR WYLIE

WILLIAM BUTLER YEATS (1865-1939): An Irish poet, Yeats
was well established as a late "romantic" poet of love and
Irish fairy tales when the twenty-three year old American
Ezra Pound came to London to learn from him and other
established poets. Yeats also learned from Pound, and his
work took a new, more "modern" direction. His marriage in
1917 to a spiritualist medium further opened his mind to a
more universal mythology, all of which made for his richly
varied poetic legacy. He was awarded the Nobel Prize for
literature in 1923.

Politics

In our time the destiny of man presents
its meaning in political terms.
THOMAS MANN

How can I, that girl standing there,
My attention fix
On Roman or on Russian
Or on Spanish politics?
Yet here's a travelled man that knows
What he talks about,
And there's a politician
That has read and thought,
And maybe what they say is true
Of war and war's alarms,
But O that I were young again
And held her in my arms!

WILLIAM BUTLER YEATS

The Lake Isle of Innisfree

I will arise and go now, and go to Innisfree,
And a small cabin build there, of clay and wattles made;
Nine bean rows will I have there, a hive for the honey bee,
And live alone in the bee-loud glade.

And I shall have some peace there, for peace comes
    dropping slow,
Dropping from the veils of the morning to where the cricket
    sings;
There midnight's all a glimmer, and noon a purple glow,
And evening full of the linnet's wings.

I will arise and go now, for always night and day
I hear lake water lapping with low sounds by the shore;
While I stand on the roadway, or on the pavements gray,
I hear it in the deep heart's core.

WILLIAM BUTLER YEATS

*DALE ZIEROTH (1946-   ) was born in Manitoba and has
lived in Winnipeg and Toronto. He has only recently begun
to publish his work, much of which recalls his prairie child-
hood and journeys. He now lives in Vancouver.*

Father

Twice he took me in his hands and shook
me like a sheaf of wheat, the way a dog shakes
a snake, as if he meant to knock out my tongue
and grind it under his heel right there
on the kitchen floor. I never remembered
what he said or the warnings he gave; she
always told me afterwards, when he
had left and I had stopped my crying. I
was eleven that year and for seven more years
I watched his friends laughing and him
with his great hands rising and falling
with every laugh, smashing down on his knees
and making the noise of a tree when it cracks

240

in winter. Together they drank chokecherry
wine and talked of the dead friends and the
old times when they were young, and because
I never thought of getting old, their
youth was the first I knew of dying.

Sunday before church he would trim
his fingernails with the hunting knife
his East German cousins had sent, the same
knife he used for castrating pigs and
skinning deer: things that had nothing
to do with Sunday. Communion once
a month, a shave every third day, a
good chew of snuff, these were the things
that helped a man to stand in the sun for
eight hours a day, to sweat through each
cold hail storm without a word, to freeze
fingers and feet to cut wood in winter, to do
the work that bent his back a little more
each day down toward the ground.

Last Christmas, for the first time, he
gave presents, unwrapped and bought
with pension money. He drinks mostly coffee
now, sleeping late and shaving every day.
Even the hands have changed: white, soft,
unused hands. Still he seems content
to be this old, to be sleeping in the middle
of the afternoon with his mouth open as if there
is no further need for secrets, as if he is
no longer afraid to call his children fools
for finding different answers, different lives.

DALE ZIEROTH

120 Miles North of Winnipeg

My grandfather came here years ago,
family of eight. In the village,
nine miles away, they knew him as
the German and they were suspicious, being
already settled. Later he was
somewhat liked; still later
forgotten. In winter everything
went white as buffalo bones and
the underwear froze on the line
like corpses. Often the youngest
was sick. Still he never thought
of leaving. Spring was always greener
than he'd known and summer had
kid-high grass with sunsets big
as God. The wheat was thick,
the log house chinked and warm.
The little English he spoke
he learned from the thin grey lady in
the one-room school, an hour away
by foot. The oldest could hunt, the youngest
could read. They knew nothing of
the world he'd left, and forgotten,
until 1914 made him an alien and
he left them on the land he'd come to,
120 miles north of Winnipeg.

DALE ZIEROTH

Index of Titles

Index of First Lines

"Here's Grandmother in here," Cousin Joy said / 46
He's five foot two and he's six feet four / 198
His boy had stolen some money from a booth / 82
His peasant parents killed themselves with toil / 19
Hold fast to dreams / 102
How can I, that girl standing there / 239
how we turn out to be related / 100

I / 143
I am the family face / 95
I am the man who gives the word / 15
I am the people – the mob – the crowd – the mass / 199
I can't find her eyes / 176
I do not think that our fathers ever met / 98
I drive my car to supermarket / 232
If I should die, think only this of me / 50
I got pocketed behind 7X-3824 / 42
I had a hippopotamus; I kept him in a shed / 22
I have always known / 156
I have known the silence of the stars and of the sea / 140
I have known you / 83
I have no respect for you / 213
I like to see it lap the miles / 72
"I'll never speak to Jamie again" – / 185
I met a traveller from an antique land / 211
I must go down to the seas again, to the lonely sea and the sky
   / 139
I never saw a moor / 71
I never thought I'd feel like this / 181
In form and feature, face and limb / 128
In former days we'd both agree / 50
in Just- / 64
I sat next the duchess at tea / 14
I saw a famous man eating soup / 200
"Is there anybody there?" said the Traveller / 69
I think a time will come when you will understand / 182
I think I am going to love it here / 31
I think I could turn and live with animals, they are so / 234
It is not growing like a tree / 106
It occurred to Marshall / 134
It's not hard to begin / 160
It took the sea a thousand years / 186
It was a summer evening / 219
It was many and many a year ago / 177
I was the last passenger of the day / 58

Snow melts / 104
Sometimes / 18
So that I would not pick the blueflag / 45
St. Agnes' Eve – Ah, bitter chill it was! / 107
Stiff as flowers / 233
Still there is a photograph of me / 214
Still to be neat, still to be drest / 106

That red fox / 29
The boy was ten years old / 65
The butterfly, the cabbage white / 90
The face of war is my face / 101
The flower-fed buffaloes of the spring / 131
The fog comes / 200
The geese flying south / 13
The great valley of Drumheller / 43
The old dog barks backward without getting up / 81
The piercing chill I feel / 53
There are many cumbersome ways to kill a man / 48
There is something in the autumn that is native to my
    blood / 56
There's a notable clan yclept Stein / 14
There was an old fellow of Tyre / 14
The rich man has his motor car / 13
The routine trickery of the examination / 202
The short night is through / 53
The soldier said / 143
The trees along this city street / 150
The tusks that clashed in mightly brawls / 93
The wind was a torrent of darkness among the gusty
    trees / 163
The year's at the spring / 51
They hurried here, as soon as you had died / 172
They say it's guarded better / 12
Things made by iron and handled by steel / 126
Things men have made with wakened hands, and put soft life
    into / 127
This I beheld, or dreamed it in a dream / 212
This is before electricity / 17
This midnight breathing / 169
Through the gate / 120
To-day we have naming of parts. Yesterday / 192
To JS/07/M/378/20
Toll no bell for me, dear Father, dear Mother / 146
To see a world in a grain of sand / 42
Twice he took me in his hands and shook / 240

Copyright Acknowledgements

Illustrations